THE QURAN'S REJECTION
OF
JESUS CHRIST AS LORD AND SAVIOR

BY REV. WILLIAM LAMPTEY

CONTENTS

INTRODUCTION

My intention in writing this book is twofold. One is to inform the believer that the Quran and Islam totally reject the God of the Bible and the message of Christ being our Lord and Savior. This book will provide scriptural references for the Christian who is aiming to reach Muslims for the Christian faith. It will also serve as a reference book for ministers of the gospel who are looking for more knowledge and information to teach their churches on the subject of Christianity and Islam.

Many Christians are fearful of sharing the gospel with their Muslim neighbors. There is the fear-of-the-unknown reaction, a fear of rejection, and the fear of being attacked for sharing the gospel. Much of these fears especially in western countries are imaginary rather than real.

We live in an era where the prophecies of the book of Daniel 12:4 are being fulfilled. "But thou, O Daniel, shut up the words, and seal the book, even to the time of the end: *many shall run to and fro, and knowledge shall be increased*".

The phrase **"Many running to and fro"** refers to the mixing up of the world's population. This further implies that the different religions and beliefs will mix up and interact with each other. Fifty to sixty years ago, virtually all Muslims used to live in their own native countries with the Christians also living in their own native countries. At that time in order to reach Muslims with the gospel, one had to travel to Muslim countries. Today, many Christians are living side-by-side with Muslims in their own respective Christian countries. It is therefore now possible to share our Christian faith with Muslims without traveling far.

We live in an era when we Christians can get knowledge on Islamic beliefs and have opportunity to share our faith with Muslims and people of other faiths.

Knowledge is power, and applied knowledge is even greater. Therefore, this book is to provide you, the Christian, with knowledge on Islam and also to encourage and motivate you to share your faith with Muslims. It is possible especially in Western Countries to share our faith with Muslims. I pray to God that as you read through this book, God will inspire faith in your heart to either share your faith with Muslims or start believing that God can use you to bring many Muslims to the saving knowledge of Christ.

Chapter 1

THE REJECTION OF THE BIBLE BY THE QURAN, ISLAM, AND MUSLIMS

The Bible is a collection of sixty-six books spanning a long period of about 1,800 years. It is divided into the Old Testament (OT) and the new Testaments (NT), the birth of Jesus Christ being the dividing line between the two. The OT basically is a historical account of God's dealing with his elected nation Israel, and central to it is God's promise of sending Christ to save all mankind. Isaiah 35 is an example of the many wonderful promises the coming Christ was to bring to mankind. Jesus Christ himself summarized the OT in Luke 24:25-27, 44-45. He classified the parts of the OT as: Law of Moses (Torah), the Prophets, the Psalms and the Scriptures. He claimed that he, Christ, was the central person of the OT scriptures thereby claiming divinity. The NT comprises of the four Gospels, Acts, the Epistles to the churches and the book of Revelation.

The Quran follows the four classifications given by Jesus on the OT. Concerning the NT the Quran acknowledges only the gospels and ignores the rest. I will explain the spiritual reasons and significance of leaving out the rest of the NT books. Sometimes, instead of using the names of the subdivisions of the OT, it just uses the title (The Book). "The Book" on other occasions refers to the gospels or the Quran itself. You have to deduce whether the Quran is referring to itself, or parts of the OT or Gospels in context of the surrounding passages.

In other words, to have a proper understanding of what the Quran teaches on the Bible, we have to examine what the Quran teaches specifically on each classification of the OT (the Torah, the Psalms, and the Prophets) and also the Gospels.

The Quran's Teachings on the Torah

We who revealed the law (to Moses): therein was guidance and light. By its standard have been judged the Jews, by the prophets who bowed (as in Islam) to Allah's will, by the rabbis and the doctors of law: for to them was entrusted the protection of Allah's book, and they were witnesses thereto: therefore fear not men, but fear me, and sell not my signs for a miserable price. If any do fail to judge by (the light of) what Allah hath revealed, they are (no better than) Unbelievers. (Surah 5:44)

We are told here that the Torah has guidance and light and by it the prophets, the rabbis, and the doctors of Law judged the Jews. Also please note from the statement that these groups of leaders were required to guard the Torah. There was no mentioning of the Torah being corrupted in this passage. Surely how could the Quran say the Jewish religious leaders guarded a corrupted Torah? When the Quran is saying the Torah has guidance and light in it, it is important to refresh our memories that the Torah was written by Moses who lived approximately 1500 BC, making it over 2,000 years old up to the time of Mohammed. Mohammed saw fit to reveal that a book that was more than 2,000 years old had guidance and light which was being guarded by the top religious leaders for more than 2,000 years. Let us look on another passage of the Quran on the Torah. "And who believe in the Revelation sent to thee, and sent before thy time, and (in their hearts) have the assurance of the Hereafter" (Surah 2:4).

In this passage, the Quran is claiming that he Mohammed, and the Muslims believe that which was revealed before (Torah and rest of the scriptures). In examining verse 4, there is no claim that the Bible has been corrupted, falsified, tampered with, changed, and so forth. It is of the highest folly for the Muslims to be told to believe in a book that is not true. Let us examine another passage in the Quran on the Law, Jesus, and the Gospel.

And in their footsteps We sent Jesus the son of Mary, confirming the Law that had come before him: We sent him the Gospel: therein was guidance and light, and confirmation of the Law that had come before him: a guidance and an admonition to those who fear Allah. (Surah 5:46)

We are told here, that the Gospels (Matthew, Mark, Luke, and John) had guidance and light and more importantly confirmed the Law. The Quran is declaring the Bible to be genuine and true. Unfortunately, when we Christians point out the above passage to the Muslims, especially their scholars, all

11

we get back from them is careless dismissal of a very obvious fact. Having established that there are passages that declare the Bible to be true, let's now find how the Quran then binds itself to the Bible so that the Muslims will believe that it is the continuation of prophets' bringing God's word to mankind. There are two words used by the Quran to achieve this. They are *"verification"* or *"confirmation"* and *"guardian."*

In the following passages we find the Quran asserting that it came to verify the books of the Bible.

O Children of Israel! call to mind the (special) favour which I bestowed on you,… And believe in what I reveal, confirming the revelation which is with you (Jews). (Surah 2:40-41)

And when there came to them a Messenger from Allah, confirming what was with them (Jews). (Surah 2:101)

And this is a Book which We have sent down, bringing blessings, and confirming (the revelations) which came before it. (Surah 6:92)

That which We have revealed to thee of the Book is the Truth,- confirming what was (revealed) before it. (Surah 35:31)

When it is said to them, "Believe in what Allah Hath sent down, "they say, "We believe in what was sent down to us:" yet they reject all besides, even if it be Truth confirming what is with them. (Surah 2:91)

It is He Who sent down to thee (step by step), in truth, the Book, confirming what went before it; and He sent down the Law (of Moses) and the Gospel (of Jesus) before this, as a guide to mankind, and He sent down the criterion (of judgment between right and wrong) (Surah 3:3-4)

As Guardian:

"To thee We sent the Scripture in truth, confirming the scripture that came before it, and guarding it in safety" (Surah 5:48).

In the above passages we find Mohammed trying desperately to cling to the Bible. He had to come out with such surahs to defend his prophethood every time he was challenged by the Christians and the Jews. Despite the Muslims reading such straightforward statements in the Quran that the Quran was revealed to verify and guard the Bible, they willfully overlook such simple assertions. Why can't over a billion souls realize something that is so simple: that you can only *verify* and *guard* over a book that is *genuine and true*?

Before someone accuses me of double standards by quoting the above Quranic passages to support the authenticity of the Bible, I am not quoting the above passages to support the validity of the Bible. I quoted them to show the double standards of Islam. Despite the above passages, there are other passages in the Quran that directly contradict them. There are many passages that attack and condemn the Jews and the Christians for changing, corrupting, concealing parts, and falsifying their holy scriptures. Below are some of these passages:

Corruption of the scriptures by the Jews

Surah 2:79 "Then woe to those who write the Book with their own hands, and then say: "This is from Allah," to traffic with it for miserable price!—Woe to them for what their hands do write, and for the gain they make thereby."

Surah 4:46 "Of the Jews there are those who displace words from their (right) places, and say: "We hear and we disobey"; and "Hear, may you not hear"; and "Ra'ina"; with a twist of their tongues and a slander to Faith."

Surah 5:41 "or it be among the Jews,- men who will listen to any lie,- will listen even to others who have never so much as come to thee. They change the words from their (right) times and places: they say."

Surah 2:75 "Can ye (o ye men of Faith) entertain the hope that they will believe in you?—Seeing that a party of them heard the Word of Allah, and perverted it knowingly after they understood it."

Surah 5:13 "But because of their breach of their covenant, We cursed them, and made their hearts grow hard; they change the words from their (right) places and forget a good part of the message that was sent them.

Corruption of the Scriptures by the Christians

From those, too, who call themselves Christians, We did take a covenant, but they forgot a good part of the message that was sent them: so we estranged them, with enmity and hatred between the one and the other, to the Day of Judgment. And soon will Allah show them what it is they have done. (Surah 5:14)

75. Christ the son of Mary was no more than an apostle; many were the apostles that passed away before him. His mother was

a woman of truth. They had both to eat their (daily) food. See how Allah doth make His signs clear to them; yet see in what ways they are deluded away from the truth!."

76. Says: "Will ye worship, besides Allah, something which hath no power either to harm or benefit you? But Allah,—He it is that heareth and knoweth all things."

77. Say: "O people of the Book! exceed not in your religion the bounds (of what is proper), trespassing beyond the truth, nor follow the vain desires of people who went wrong in times gone by,- who misled many, and strayed (themselves) from the even way. (Surah 5:75-77)

69. It is the wish of a section of the People of the Book to lead you astray. But they shall lead astray (Not you), but themselves, and they do not perceive!

70. Ye People of the Book! Why reject ye the Signs of Allah, of which ye are (Yourselves) witnesses?

71. Ye People of the Book! Why do ye clothe Truth with false-hood, and conceal the Truth, while ye have knowledge? (Surah 3:69-71)

The above passages are serious charges and present a blanket condemnation of all Jewish and Christian communities throughout the ages. The passages of condemnations listed above are only a few examples found in the Quran.

Mohammed could hardly open his mouth without condemning the Jews and the Christians for what he saw as their altering the word of God.

Over the years I have seen Christian tracts and pamphlets trying to quote the Quran passages that claim to verify the Bible. They aim to convince and convict the Muslims that the Bible is true and authentic. I don't believe that much is achieved through that course of action. Most of these tracts come from the Middle East where obviously the Christians can't speak their minds openly and are constantly looking over their shoulders. The best they can do is to appeal to the Muslims that the Quran claims to verify and guard the Bible. Because the Christians can't say openly that it is the Quran which could be wrong, they adopt this position and stand in danger of being accused of double standards.

For every verse of the Quran that claims to verify and guard the scriptures, there are countless others that inform Muslims that the Bible is unreliable, corrupted by the Jews and Christians. Mohammed, by the power given to him by the spirit of Allah, has supernaturally blinded Muslims and held them spellbound. If I am wrong, how does one explain such blatant misinformation to so many people?

One foot of Mohammed, the prophet of Allah, is planted firmly in the Bible, and the other foot is out. Mohammed desperately needed a witness to back his claim as a prophet. No one in the world lives on an isolated island by himself. We all need witnesses in our life, especially a person like Mohammed, who sought to start a new religion. Mohammed, by his many assertions that he came to verify and guard the Bible, was actually seeking scriptures to authenticate his claims. He knew that before he was born the Bible had taken root in many nations, and for him to be accepted as true prophet of God, the Bible must be seen to be supporting his claims. This he did very successfully and cleverly. I personally believe that it is his one foot in the Bible that has convinced many Muslims that he is a true prophet of God.

The Bible was the only religious book that had taken deep root in the world. It was the only book that declared unequivocally the existence of God, heaven, angels, Satan and Hell. For someone to come into the world starting a new religion and talking about God without reference to the Bible would have appeared very strange and highly suspicious. Satan is not that daft. Not many Muslims would have followed him if he had come talking about God without referring to the Bible. Mohammed should have also produced the original Bible so that people could compare it to the ones he was busy claiming the Christians had corrupted. He should have further made sure that he had in his possession and control every single manuscript of the Bible from every corner of the world at his time. He should have *also* had in his possession all correspondence and writings between all Jews and Christians from the time of Moses, to Jesus, to his own time. Spreading accusations is cheap—anyone can do it if the person doesn't have to provide a single shred of evidence.

Mohammed, by his charges that the Bible had been corrupted, was a serious affront to the great and dreadful God of Israel. He accused God of total incompetence and negligence. His claims meant that no single prophet's writings existed intact. The great and dreaded prophets of Israel suddenly had no genuine writings left behind for mankind except, of course, what Mohammed told the people. What mattered was what he told the people about the prophets, not what the prophets left behind or said God had told them. When I ponder on his claims concerning the prophets' writings, it sends shivers through me. How could one man make such audacious claims?

In the over-twenty years I have been trying to share my Christian faith with Muslims, I am amazed at the intensity of the attacks and ridicule of the Bible by Muslims. From the youngest Muslim child to the oldest grandparents, they never cease to vilify the Bible. Whether they are moderate Muslims or fanatical ones, once they see the Bible in your hands and you try to tell them about it, they will ridicule it by charging that it has been corrupted. Because of the continuous charges in the Quran that "they" (Jews and Christians) have corrupted the Holy Scriptures, the Muslims' subconscious minds are infused with this monstrous trickery. The Muslims totally ignore the numerous passages of Mohammed claiming to verify and guard the Bible with the Quran.

Many people accuse and attack the Bible in every nation but without any doubt, I firmly believe that Islam and the Muslims by far top the list. They are relentless in this ignorant pursuit. I have hardly met any Muslim who, when discussing with Christians spiritual issues, could say six sentences without attacking the Bible. They despise God's Holy Book. It is very frightening to observe their onslaught on the Bible. To me it is like they are under a spell. A fair majority of Muslims don't care how Christians feel when they slander their holy book.

Both moderate and fanatical Muslims continuously attack the Bible. The only difference between the two groups is that the moderates will say the same things in a gentler way. I have always deliberated on the reasons why Muslims are so determined to declare that the Bible has been changed. Why can't they understand that whether the Bible has been changed or not is no proof that the Quran is true?

I find Islam to be totally hypercritical in their attitude towards the Bible. They are always quick to open their mouth and declare that they believe in all the prophets, and yet when you read them the writings of the prophets they are quick to denounce them as corrupted.

I have had hundreds of encounters with Muslims on the validity of the Bible. While they use varied approaches, the end result is the same violent refutation of the Bible. Below are a few of some of the encounters I have had with them.

I once tried to share the gospel with four Algerians in East London. They kept charging that the Bible has been changed, falsified, and so forth. I then asked the first person whether he had ever read just one complete chapter of the Bible before. He replied "no." I then asked the second and the third person the same question, and they both replied "no." When I repeated the question to the fourth person he stiffened up and became angry, asking me why I was asking them that question. I replied that I wanted to be sure that they have read the scriptures. He said I was only asking them because I was only trying to prove to them that they were fools. I quickly reminded him that that word "fools" did not come from my lips but from his. He threatened me, and I quickly had to leave the scene remembering Jesus admonition in Matthew 10:22-23.

I traveled a few months after that incident to Washington, DC. I narrated the whole scenario with the four Algerians in East London to a Moroccan Muslim I tried to share my faith with. I asked him who was speaking through those four Algerians when they kept charging that the Bible had been corrupted when they had not even read just one chapter of the Bible. I asked him whether it was God or the devil speaking through them. He laughed and said obviously it must be the devil. He even joked and said that God is not the author of foolishness. He said no one should condemn something that he had never examined. I ask you the reader the same question. Every time the Muslims open their mouth and attack the Bible, saying that it has been corrupted without reading the Bible let alone checking it, who is speaking through them, God or the devil? Below is another encounter I had with a Muslim on a train.

He saw me reading the Bible on a train and the following dialogue took place.

Mr. Muslim: Is that the Bible you are reading?
Mr. Christian: That's correct.
Mr. Muslim: Are you then a Christian?
Mr. Christian: That's correct.
Mr. Muslim: Show me in the Bible where it says that Jesus is God or divine.
Mr. Christian: I opened John 1:1 to show him the verse "In the beginning was the Word and the word was with God and

the word was God." It is Jesus being called the Word and the Word (Jesus) was God.

Mr. Muslim: No, Jesus is not God. That cannot be true.

Mr. Christian: But you asked me to show it to you in the Bible that Jesus is God. I have shown it to you. In verse 3, it also says that all things were created by Him. If you want me to show you more passages I can.

Mr. Muslim: I don't believe it because you Christians have changed God's word.

Mr. Christian: Shouldn't your scholars produce the original Bible for us Christians to see?

Mr. Muslim: It is hidden in the archive at Rome by the Pope. He reached his destination and left the train speaking things he had no knowledge of.

Another trickery the Muslims use to attack the Bible is the issue of "different versions of the Bible." This angle of attack on the Bible is very popular with Muslims. They love to use it. They will come to you when they see the Bible in your hands, pretending they want to hear you read it to them. They will then ask:

Mr. Muslim: Is that the Bible in your hands?

Mr. Christian: Yes, it is

Mr. Muslim: Which version is that?

Mr. Christian: It is the King James Version (but there are the NIV, Good News, etc.).

Mr. Muslim: Which of the versions is the true one (implying there are false ones)?

Mr. Christian: I don't understand your question. We don't have true and false ones.

Mr. Muslim: We Muslims only have one Quran, which has never been changed. You Christians have many Bibles. We want to know which one is true so that we can believe it (Do you remember King Herod and the wise men in Matthew 2:1-12?)

Mr. Christian: The different versions are only different translations from the manuscripts.

Mr. Muslim: We want to know which of these versions the genuine one is (totally ignoring the simple statement by Mr. Christian).

I have repeatedly encountered this particular dialogue with so many Muslims from different nations. It is as if someone rehearses with them what to say in their various mosques. What they are really doing is mocking the Bible. Many Muslims know that the different versions of the Bible are only merely different translations from the manuscripts. Despite this simple knowledge, they wickedly pretend that they don't know this and constantly waste the Christians' time. For the reader who is unaware of this struggle between Muslims and the Christians on the issue of the different versions of the Bible, I offer this thought.

There are minor differences in the versions because it is not always possible to translate with 100 percent accuracy from one language to another. Certain words may have more than one meaning in the original language. Remember also that the Bible is a big book. Some of the translations are also modern English, and some are old English. Similar problems also exist with the Quran. If you pick two translations of the English Quran you will not find every word agreeing with each other. The Arabic is the same, but the translations to English are never word-by-word the same. Just as some translations are considered by some Christians to be better than others, so do some Muslims consider certain translations better than others. I have always had two translations of the Quran. Sometimes the numbering of the verses does not even agree. What is verse 93 in one translation could be verse 94 or 92 in another translation. This lack of agreement in the numbering of the verses has always caused problems for me when I am writing. Sometimes one forgets which translation one is using, and the secretary may type different verses from another translation.

Recently a personal Muslim friend of mine read in the Quran that Allah promised to guard the Quran against corruption. He then asked me many times whether God made a similar promise in the Bible to protect it from corruption. Let us examine a few scriptures in answer to my Muslim friend.

"The grass withereth, the flower fadeth: but the word of God shall stand forever" (Isaiah 40:8). The same verse is quoted in 1 Peter 1: 25. A stronger word to use is "endureth." The phrases "stand forever" and "endureth" inform us that the Bible will be challenged, ridiculed, mocked, and ceaseless efforts made to destroy it, but it will prevail over all his enemies. Other very assuring words of promise are found in the Bible, such as Psalm 119:89, **"Forever, O Lord thy word is settled in heaven."** The pages of the Bible we Christians hold today are opened up in the very presence of Almighty God in heaven.

Jesus assured us many times in the New Testament that the scriptures will all be fulfilled, stand the test of time, honored, obeyed, and loved. Listen to his assuring words in the following scriptures:

"Think not that I am come to destroy the law, or the prophets: I am not come to destroy, but to fulfil. For verily I say unto you, till heaven and earth pass, one jot or one title shall in no wise pass from the law, till all be fulfilled." Matthew 5:17-18

And this gospel of the kingdom shall be preached in the entire world for a witness unto all nations; and then shall the end come.... Heaven and earth shall pass away, but my words shall not pass away. (Matthew 24:14, 35)

If he called them gods, unto whom the word of God came, and the scripture cannot be broken. (John 10:35)

At the close of the Bible we have a clear warning for all those who will try to rewrite God's word. Note the following scripture verses:

For I testify unto every man that heareth the words of the prophecy of this book, if any man shall add unto these things, God shall add unto him the plagues that are written in this book: And if any man shall take away from the words of the book of this prophecy, God shall take away his part out of the book of life, and out of the holy city, and from the things which are written in this book. (Revelation 22:18-19)

Let us now examine other evidences in support of the truthfulness of the Bible.

Scriptures that New Testament writers and Jesus quoted directly from the Old Testament

The New Testament writers quoted many times from the Old Testament. Using the book of Matthew as an example, let us examine the first five chapters for direct Old Testament quotations.

Matthew 1

In this chapter we are given the genealogy of Christ through Joseph (the adopted father of Christ) to Abraham. All the major characters of the Old Testament are listed there. This assures us that the characters we read about in the Old Testament are true. Isaiah 7:14 is directly quoted in verse 23.

Matthew 2

Micah 5:2 and Genesis 49:10 are quoted in the first six verses. Hosea 11:1 is quoted in verse 15 and in verse 18, Jeremiah 31:15 is quoted.

Matthew 3

Isaiah 40:3 is quoted in verse 2.

Matthew 4

Jesus quoted Deuteronomy 8:3 in answer to the devil's temptation in verse 4. The devil quoted Psalm 91:11,12 and tried to put a different interpretation on it in verse 6. Jesus again replied to him with verse 7, quoting directly from Deuteronomy 6:16. Satan again tried to trick Jesus in verses 8 and 9, and Jesus rebuffed his lies with a direct quote from Deuteronomy 6:13. Isaiah 9:1-2 is quoted in verses 15 and 16.

Matthew 5

The book of Leviticus and Deuteronomy are quoted a few times in this chapter. Most Bibles have direct quotes of the Old Testament in the New Testament highlighted, and if you go through the rest of the book of Matthew and the other NT books you will find numerous direct quotes of the Old Testament in them. Let's now examine the significance of these direct quotes.

It is clear that the writers of the New Testament had in their possession the Old Testament books and knew them. They used the Old Testament scriptures to substantiate the claims of Christ and their testimonies about him. At the time of the New Testament writers, the Old Testament was widely distributed around many nations and was read regularly in many synagogues. Read through 2 Peter 1:15-21 and catch the joy that flowed in Peter's heart just before his death when he narrated some of the wonders they experienced in the presence of the Lord and the scriptures they had to support those experiences. The phrase he used to describe the Old Testament scriptures—"a more sure word of prophecy," sums it up. *Peter said the Old Testament scriptures were of more relevance to the disciples than seeing Jesus' face transfigured as the sun.* Think about it! What a statement.

From the time of Adam and Eve the world had waited for the coming of the promised deliverer (her Seed) to deliver mankind from the clutches of Satan. Men have intensely longed for this deliverer but never knew when, where, and in what manner he would come. There was a big cloud of darkness covering the coming of this blessed Savior. Nobody knew the how and when of his coming except the prophets; and even among the prophets, no one prophet had the full picture. Each prophet prophesied about a certain aspect of his life. It was against this background that Peter said that the prophets' prophesies were of more weight than seeing Jesus' body transfigured.

The quotation of the Old Testament scriptures in the New Testament is one of the strongest evidence of the validity of the Bible. It is clear that the Old Testament being held today by both the Jews and the Christians is valid. As the New Testament confirms the Old Testament so does the Old Testament also confirm the New Testament. I plead with you, the Christian reader, to reflect on and study these Old Testament quotations in the New Testament. This is one of the many important tools you can use to share the gospel with your Muslim friendly neighbor who would sit with you and listen. *It is important to remember that both the Jew and the Christian carry the same Old Testament scriptures today.* The majority of the Jews have never accepted Jesus as the Savior up to today. There is no way they are going to hold a world conference with the Christians to change the word and rewrite it. It had never happened in history and will never happen.

If you are a Muslim reading this book, I appeal to you to seriously consider this point I am making. Please don't harden your heart. Yield to reasoning and allow the Holy Spirit to open your heart to the truth about this simple fact. You have read many times in the Quran that the Bible has been changed by the Jews and Christians. You have heard it from the mouth of many Muslims continuously, and you yourself have said it many times. But it is a lie. As long as you believe this lie you will never seriously consider or believe anything the Bible says. Just as Saddam Hussein said during the Gulf War that his battle with the allied forces was going to be the mother of all battles when he had inadequate resources to fight, so is your belief, that the Bible has been corrupted, is the mother of all lies.

This lie is so huge that its consequences are unimaginable. It is so simple a lie and yet so destructive. It will damn your soul for eternity. Please be bold and take a step of faith and open the pages of the Bible. Don't be afraid of other Muslims who will threaten you. If you have to flee your home, town, or city and even country to search the pages of the Bible on this simple fact, please do. Jesus has warned you in Matthew 10:28, "And fear not them which kill the body, but are not able to kill the soul: but rather fear him which is able to destroy both soul and body in hell." Your soul's safety is more important than anything else. There are many things I can point out to you that God's word cannot be changed, but there is enough evidence in examining the Old Testament quotations in the New Testament. A study of the passages can open your eyes to the numerous prophecies about Jesus in the Old Testament. Backed by the grace of God you may fall in love with the blessed Savior your religion has rejected and despised for so long. May God grant you his grace to recognize him and accept him.

To the Christian reader there are other angles I use to answer the Muslim's charge that the Bible has been changed. There are too many to include in this book. Below is a typical example I often use. It may help you to formulate your own strategies. Listen to the dialogue between Mr. Christian and Mr. Muslim.

Mr. Christian: Can I share the Bible with you?

Mr. Muslim: How can you share the Bible with me when it has been changed many times?

Mr. Christian: When was it changed? Was it before the Prophet of Allah, Mohammed, or after him?

Mr. Muslim: After Mohammed (or sometimes before—some Muslims are unsure).

Mr. Christian: Do Christians today believe in the Father, the Son, and the Holy Spirit?

Mr. Muslim: Yes, though you believe in the Father, the Son, and the Holy Spirit, it is not true. There is nothing like that. There is no God but Allah, and Mohammed is His Prophet.

Mr. Christian: So you are aware that Christians today believe in the Triune God?

Mr. Muslim: That belief is a lie.

Mr. Christian: Do you know that the Quran and Mohammed were busy warning the Christians to stop worshipping the Triune God? Clearly the Christians at the time of Mohammed believed in the Triune God.

Mr. Muslim: Yes the Quran warned them to stop saying the word "three" in **Surah 4:171-172 "and say not three, desist it is better for you."**

Mr. Christian: If according to your own mouth the Christians today believe in the Triune God and so did the Christians during the time of Mohammed, where is the changing of God's words that you complain about?

Mr. Muslim: We believe you have changed God's word. There is no God but Allah. He then walked away.

I undertook this dialogue with a young Muslim and I have had similar discussions with many other Muslims. Below is another dialogue I often employ in my preaching to Muslims.

Mr. Christian: Can we talk about the Bible?

Mr. Muslim: Your Bible has been changed.

Mr. Christian: Can we reason together to find how the Bible has been changed? Do you know how many Bibles are in the whole of London or can anyone count them?

Mr. Muslim: No, I don't know the number, neither can anyone count them

Mr. Christian: Then is it possible for anyone to enter every house, wardrobe, cabinet, attic, drawer, basement, and church to collect all the Bibles in London and destroy them, rewrite them, and redistribute them?

Mr. Muslim: No, this is not possible.

Mr. Christian: Could anybody do that in London 100 years ago?

Mr. Muslim: No, I don't think so; it wouldn't be possible at that time.

Mr. Christian: What about 500 years ago, would it be possible at that time?

Mr. Muslim: No.

Mr. Christian: What about 1,000 years ago, would it have been possible then?

Mr. Muslim : No it was not possible.

Mr. Christian: What about 1,500 years ago, would it have been possible then?

Mr. Muslim: No, I have already told you it was not possible.

Mr. Christian: Before mass printing existed, what about the thousand of manuscripts scattered all over the world in different museums, churches, and state buildings? What about thousands of biblical quotations inscribed in all churches, schools, on top of tombs, in Christian letters and literature, and so forth? Have you really thought about what you are saying? What about Jesus' warning you that for every careless word we speak we will give account of at the Day of Judgment?

Mr. Muslim: We believe the Quran, and it tells us that the Bible has been tampered with and that settles it. You Christians have changed the book. Allah is great.

He then walks away.

Over the years I have used this approach to tackle the charge of corruption of the Bible by Muslims and other skeptics. Many times it works, but occasionally when the Muslims perceive where you are heading towards, they will try to bluff and say to you that the Bible can be changed within a locality. But on the whole they know the point I am trying to make is valid and true.

I would like to caution the Christian readers. I am not providing you with fixed ideas that you will get every Muslim you approach saved. If reasoning alone could get Muslims saved, millions would have been saved throughout the world. I believe as hard as it is, Christians have made many attempts to reason with Muslims. The Bible is very clear on the nature of the spiritual conflict we are involved in. It says in Ephesians 6:12, "We wrestle not against flesh and blood, but against principalities, against powers, against the rulers of the darkness of this world, against spiritual darkness in high places." When you are dealing with Muslims, you are dealing with the number one enemy of Christ's kingdom.

31

Chapter 2

THE QURAN'S REJECTION OF THE TRIUNE GOD – THE FATHER, THE SON, AND THE HOLY SPIRIT

O people of the Book! Commit no excesses in your religion: Nor say of Allah aught but the truth. Christ Jesus the son of Mary was (no more than) an apostle of Allah, and His Word, which He bestowed on Mary, and a spirit proceeding from Him: so believe in Allah and His apostles. Say not "Trinity": desist: it will be better for you: for Allah is one Allah. Glory is to Him: (far exalted is He) above having a son. To Him belong all things in the heavens and on earth. And enough is Allah as a Disposer of affairs. (Surah 4:171)

This passage is filled with charges of corruption, threatenings, and violence against Christians. The rejection of the Triune God of the Bible is centered on the rejection of Christ's claims as more than a messenger or prophet. Please note the violence in the phrase "desist it is better for you." I don't believe it is only the spiritual punishment after judgment day that he is referring to here. Remember, Mohammed had a ruthless army that eventually silenced all his enemies.

72. They do blaspheme who say: "(Allah) is Christ the son of Mary," But said Christ: "O Children of Israel! Worship Allah, my Lord and your Lord." Whoever joins with other gods with Allah—Allah will forbid the garden, and the Fire will be his abode. There will for the wrong doers be no one to help.

73. They do blaspheme who say: Allah is one of three in a Trinity: for there is no god except one Allah. If they desist not from their word of (blasphemy), verily a grievous penalty will befall the blasphemers among them. (Surah 5:72-73)

Again in this verse before the Godhead (Trinity) is denounced and Christ is first stripped of his deity. The word "desist" appears again followed by a painful chastisement which I believe includes Mohammed's threat to send in an army to destroy the Christian communities. He and his successors did that successfully among many Middle East countries. The effect of the two above surahs has eternally marred the relationship between Christians and Muslims. How could Muslims read the above surahs regularly and not breed contempt in their hearts against the Christian infidels who are filling the world with their blasphemous doctrines of Christ being Lord and Savior? If I am wrong, then how does one explain the continuous hatred against the Coptic Christians in Egypt and the murderous activities of Bokum Haram in Nigeria? What about the continuous hatred against the western countries who predominantly are Christians? How are the Muslims going to enforce this "desist" decree if they are not to use force or Jihad?

2. He to whom belongs the dominion of the heavens and the earth: no son has He begotten, nor has He a partner in his dominion: it is He who created all things, and ordered them in due proportions."

3. Yet have they taken, besides him, gods that can create nothing but are themselves created; that have no control or hurt or good to themselves; nor can they control death nor life nor resurrection. (Surah 25:2-3)

In these verses the word "three" is not mentioned. We have instead "partner" and "gods." They are all denounced, and we are told that they have no power either to do good or evil.

"Allah has said 'Take not (for worship) two gods: for he is just One Allah, then fear Me (and Me alone)" (Surah 16:51). In this verse instead of the usual words like partners, associates, Gods, or sons and daughters, two gods are specifically mentioned.

"Allah forgiveth not that partners should be set up with Him; *but He forgiveth anything else, to whom He pleaseth;* to set up partners with Allah is to devise *a sin Most heinous indeed"* (Surah 4:48). Take note of the phrase "devise a sin most heinous indeed." Also take note of the general tone of these surahs. They are not just informing of the absence of the trinity but threatening to those who believe them, that is, the Christians. I cannot tell or count how many times Muslims have quoted the above surah to oppose my preaching of the gospel. It is while I am editing this book that the depth and the seriousness of this surah struck me. Just take a moment and reflect on the phrase **"but he forgiveth anything else to whom he pleaseth."** This verse has very serious implications within the Christian and Muslim debate. According to this surah, Allah would rather forgive persons like Hitler, Stalin, or Osama Bin Laden and many other notorious characters who had been responsible for the deaths of millions. The Christians who believe that Jesus is Lord and divine are committing a sin most heinous indeed that cannot be forgiven. Can you join me in thinking this implication through? Can you see with me the near impossibility of convincing the Muslims of the divinity of Jesus?

If a Muslim man has believed these verses all his lifetime and believes in them, how on earth can one convince him that Jesus is divine in addition to God the Father? I believe the existence of these verses in the Quran is one of the many reasons that Muslims do not accept Christ's divinity. Muslims have been brainwashed to the highest order through these surahs in rejecting the deity of Christ. I believe that you the Christian who desire to share your faith with Muslims should seriously take these surahs continously in prayer to break their control over the minds of the Muslims you desire to reach. Let us now examine what the Bible teaches on this great subject.

The passages from the Bible are too numerous. I will pick a handful from both testaments.

And God said, Let *us* make man in *our image,* after *our likeness:* and let them have dominion over the fish of the sea, and over the fowl of the air, and over the cattle, and over all the earth, and over every creeping thing that creepeth upon the earth the fish of the sea, and over the fowl of the air, and over the cattle, and over all the earth, and over every creeping thing that creepeth upon the earth. (Genesis 1:26)

The *us* in this verse stands for the Trinity: the Father, the Son, and the Holy Spirit. *Our* also is plural which stands for the Trinity. But the word *image* should have been images if the Father, the Son, and the Holy Spirit were three separate Gods independent of each other. The same thing applies to the word **likeness**—again likeness is used instead of likenesses. Words are important in life. Words describe what is there. In this verse, we are informed both about the plurality of the Trinity and its unity. Because this is a spiritual subject man has a will and man will exercise his/her will in either accepting God's word or rejecting it. Many times when one points out Genesis 1:26 to the Muslim, they either look away or explain it away that the Bible is speaking about "plurality of majesty"; thereby the Muslims exercise their wills in rejecting the plain written word of God. For you, the Christian reader, when you point out this verse to them, your job is complete. They have a choice to accept or reject the scripture. You don't have to fret if they reject the word and give another meaning to the scriptures.

The Spirit of the Lord GOD [is] upon me; because the LORD hath anointed me to preach good tidings unto the meek; he hath sent me to bind up the brokenhearted, to proclaim liberty to the captives, and the opening of the prison to [them that are] bound; (Isaiah 61:1)

The Spirit (one person of the Trinity), of the Lord God (the second person) is upon me (the third person). Jesus quoted this verse in Luke 4 to tell the Jews that he is the "me" in this verse. In other words he is the fulfillment of that verse. The

Jews got mad because they understood Jesus clearly from this verse that he was claiming to be that divine Messiah who was to come, and they, like the Muslims of today, would not have it. They were ready to throw him down the pinnacle of the temple. But thank God for Jesus' supernatural power; he passed through the midst of them and they could not lay their hands on him for his time had not yet come. When you look at the work which that person who called himself (me) is to do in the world in that verse and the following three verses, clearly that person is God or divine. We have all the three divine persons in that single verse in Isaiah 61:1.

18And Jesus came and spake unto them, saying, All power is given unto me in heaven and in earth.

19 Go ye therefore, and teach all nations, baptizing them in the name of the Father, and of the Son, and of the Holy. (Matthew 28:18-19)

Let's examine these instructions from Jesus to the disciples after His resurrection. Just imagine according to Allah and Islam that there is no Father or Holy Ghost; this phrase "the Father, the Son, and the Holy Ghost" would be totally meaningless for Jesus to have said them. Imagine if according to Islam it is only the Father who is God and no Son and no Holy Spirit, then instructions of Jesus would have meant baptizing them in the name of the Father who is God, in the name of the Son who is not God, and in the name of the Holy Spirit which does not exist or at best exists but is not God. Clearly, Mohammed and Jesus are speaking directly opposite things and not from the same camp. One of them is lying to us. We the human race has a responsibility to find out who is doing the lying so that we do not end up being destroyed.

"The grace of the Lord Jesus Christ, and the love of God, and the communion of the Holy Ghost, [be] with you all. Amen" (2 Corinthians 13:14). Again in this verse we have all the three divine persons mentioned in one verse. I want to particularly dwell on the communion or the fellowship of the Holy Spirit. When Paul penned this scripture, Mohammed was yet to be born by about 500 years. Paul definitely was not speaking about Mohammed who was to come 500 years later. He was referring to the Holy Spirit; who was already working with the disciples instructing, teaching, and directing the disciples in their missionary activities. Go through the Acts of the Apostles and note the passages where the Holy Spirit gave instructions to the disciples about what to do. Many times in the Acts of the Apostles, he gave and spoke commands just like any person would do. For further reading on the Holy Spirit, please refer to chapter 12 of this book.

In all the major differences and conflicts between Christianity and Islam, this subject is of the most importance. If a religion gets the identity of God or the Creator of heaven and earth wrong, everything else will be wrong. To have the identity wrong is to have a false god, a false religion, and to worship the devil. There are two objects of worship: the true God or the devil. These are the only two powers that men worship. Anything worshipped other than the true God will eventually lead to the worshipping of Satan. If the worshipping of the one person Allah constantly repeated in the Quran is the truth, then the Christian faith of worshipping the Triune God is false, and they are worshipping Satan—and vice versa. There can be no compromise on this. Logic and reasoning demands that only one concept of God can be right. The others are wrong and satanic. If you, the reader, is among those who believe, teach, think, or say that the Muslim and the Christian worship the same God, I strongly appeal to you to change your mind. *Allah is not the Triune God of the Bible and the Triune God of the Bible is not Allah.* The two are deadly enemies and everywhere they meet there is continuous conflict and war. Each is seeking to win the hearts of men. Let us now examine which of these two concepts of deity is plausible and correct, starting with Allah.

I ponder on the facts that the Quran asserts continuously that Allah has existed from eternity alone without a partner, friend, associate, or son. I see him as a very lonely god; totally and exclusively lonely. I certainly do not want to worship such a god. Allah is also filled with intense hatred of having partners, friends, and sons. This intense hatred is violent. Allah doesn't share anything with another deity and does not want to share anything with another deity. Although he claims to have created the heavens and the earth according to Islam, he didn't have anyone to love neither did anyone love him. *How could a god from eternity who never had a friend, associate, son, companion, who never knew the joy of loving others or being loved suddenly create my soul and wants me to love him?* How could he give me love to love him when he himself had no love for any other from eternity? I believe such a god has to be very proud, unapproachable, and autocratic and could be questioned for his justice, fairness, and righteousness. Is it any wonder when you read the Quran you are constantly reminded that Allah does what he pleases, wills for man what he wants, and does not give an account to anyone for his actions? Contrast the character of Allah of the Quran and the God of the Bible. The difference is as big as the distance between heaven and hell.

Just listen to the God of the Bible speaking in Isaiah 1:18. "Come now, and let us reason together, saith the LORD: though your sins be as scarlet, they shall be as white as snow; though they be red like crimson, they shall be as wool." Where do you find in the Quran Allah pleading with men like in Isaiah 1:18? All Allah does in the Quran is give instruction and demand total prostration and submission. If you doubt me, do a study on Allah declaring his powers in the Quran.

Allah definitely has neither a partner nor an associate; but Yahweh, the God of Israel and the God of the Bible, definitely has a partner or associate. He doesn't hate him and is not ashamed of him. Listen to him declaring his love and affection for his partner in Zechariah 13:7

Awake, O sword, against my shepherd, and against *the man [that is] my fellow, saith the LORD of hosts:* smite the shepherd, and the sheep shall be scattered: and I will turn mine hand upon the little ones.

The prophet Zechariah says that God has a partner, but Mohammed says that Allah has no partner. Clearly the two men are in opposite camps concerning the identity of God.

"Thou lovest righteousness, and hatest wickedness: *there-fore God, thy God*, hath anointed thee with the oil of glad-ness above thy fellows" (Psalms 45:7). This is one of the great Psalms about Jesus in the Bible. It is the Father speaking here about his son Jesus Christ. That portion of this Psalm is quoted in Hebrews 1. According to the last verse in this Psalm, the Father would make sure that Jesus' name would be remembered praised, and worshipped throughout eternity by all generations. In verses 6 and 7, the Father calls Jesus God and goes on to say that He the Father is still the God of Jesus because Jesus came from his bosom.

Let us look at the phrase **"therefore God, thy God,"** in verse 7. Two persons being called directly God; the first person is Jesus and the second person there is the Father. The Father here is called the first God—the God of Jesus. Many people are confused about the relationship between Jesus and the Father even among the Christians. The Father is always the God of Jesus because Jesus originated from inside the Father (John 1:18). This knowledge is very important to eliminate con-fusion in many people's minds. Christ, before he was incar-nated, existed and lived inside the bosom of God the Father. That is why he always called the Father "my God and my Father." The Bible always calls God the Father "the God and the Father of Jesus" (Ephesians 1:3) but never the other way around. Jesus is never called the God of the Father. Jesus always referred to himself as coming from God. There was a time when Christ was hidden inside the Father until, according to Hebrews 1:6, the Father revealed Jesus to creation and he asked all the angels of God to worship him. Then in verse 8 he says, *"but unto the Son he (Father saith) thy throne o God is forever and ever."* The Father called the Son God in verse 8 and says that he has a throne from eternity.

According to the translator of the Quran I'm using, he commented in one of the pages that the death of Jesus and the birth of Jesus are shrouded in mystery. As an Islamic scholar and commentator, he knows most of the biblical account of the birth of Jesus but appears to have rejected them. He has chosen rather to uphold the quranic accounts that are inconclusive and confusing.

Listen again to the Father speaking in Matthew 3:16-17

And Jesus, when he was baptized, went up straightway out of the water: and, lo, the heavens were opened unto him, and he saw the Spirit of God descending like a dove, and lighting upon him: And lo a voice from heaven, saying, This is my beloved Son, in whom I am well pleased.

What a wonderful expression of deep love and totally opposite to Allah in the Quran. Listen also to the Son speaking about his Father in John 14:31, "But that the world may know that I love the Father; and as the Father gave me commandment, even so I do. Arise, let us go hence." Also John 17:24 says, "For thou loved me before the foundation of the world." Muslims choose to believe in Allah, who is and has been lonely from eternity and hates the idea of having a son or partner, above the Triune God with wonderful expressions of love. I suspect the real reason is that most people do not stop to think and reflect about what they believe in their religions, primarily because the mind is paralyzed when it comes to spiritual issues.

One of the reasons given in the Quran why Allah does not have a son or partner is the issue of sharing his power. Let us take a look at some of the Quran passages on this issue.

91. No son did Allah beget, nor is there any god along with Him: (if there were many gods), behold, each god would have taken away what he had created, and some would have lorded it over others! Glory to Allah. (He is free) from the (sort of) things they attribute to Him!

92. He knows what is hidden and what is open: too high is He for the partners they attribute to Him! (Surah 23:91-92)

22. If there were, in the heavens and the earth, other gods besides Allah, there would have been confusion in both! but glory to Allah, the Lord of the Throne: (High is He) above what they attribute to Him!

23. He cannot be questioned for His acts, but they will be questioned (for theirs).

24. Or have they taken for worship (other) gods besides him? Say, "Bring your convincing proof: this is the Message of those with me and the Message of those before me." But most of them know not the Truth, and so turn away. (Surah 21:22-24)

These passages in the Quran are scandalously believed by over one billion men and women as factually correct, revealed knowledge. The statements in the Quran that belief in the

Triune God would lead to fighting and disorder totally ignore the character and nature of God and lack understanding on the subject. Christians do not worship three separate gods who are independent of one another; neither does the Bible teach that. The Bible teaches one God in three persons, who is referred to as the Father, the Son, and the Holy Spirit. The Triune God is spiritually bonded together to make one God. They are mutually dependent on each other; they are in perfect unity bonded by unspeakable love. They shared the same glory: "I have glorified thee on the earth: I have finished the work which thou gavest me to do. And now, O Father, glorify thou me with thine own self with the glory which I had with thee before the world was" (John 17:4-5). In addition they had been together from eternity with Christ and the Holy Spirit dwelling in the bosom of the Father. John 1:18 and John 15:26 explain the bond between the Father, Jesus, and the Holy Spirit.

The only begotten Son who is in the bosom of the Father (John 1:18)

But when the comforter is come, whom I will send unto you from the Father, even the Spirit of truth. (John 15:26)

Many times Christ said that he and the Father are one (John 17). He also said in John 17:24 that the Father has loved him before the foundation of the world. All these passages are in direct contradiction to the Quran verses above that teach that Allah being more than one person would result in upheaval.

There is no iniquity within the Godhead; they have never fought and neither will they ever fight. How can they ever fight when you have the following promises in the Bible such as found in John 3:35; John 4:34 and John 8:29?

44

The Father loveth the Son, and hath given all things into his hand.

Jesus saith unto them, My meat is to do the will of him that sent me. and to finish his work.

And he that sent me is with me: the Father hath not left me alone; for I do always those things that please him.

It is true God can't share his glory with idols, images of idols, and all the numerous objects of worship because they didn't create the world and they are not gods. But when it comes to Yahweh, there are three persons involved and they cannot deny each other. Let us now examine other evidences in support of the Bible.

The Names of God

All the names of God without exception are always plural but united. *The Bible does not teach one person one God as it is taught in Islam.* The names of God—*Yaweh, Jehovah, Adonai*, are all plural; even *Elohim*, the word translated as God in the English language itself is plural but united. All the prophets testified in their writings and prophecies that there is more than one person in the Godhead.

The Appearances of God (Theophanous)

The Bible is full of instances when the heavens were opened to the prophets and to the holy men. In many of them, they recorded seeing more than one divine personality. One is in Isaiah 6:3, "And one cried unto another, and said holy, holy,

holy, is the Lord of hosts: the whole earth is full of his glory." There is threefold praise of the holiness of God: One to the Father, one to the Son, and one to the Holy Spirit. In verse 8, they asked Isaiah "whom shall I send and who will *go for us*?" The Godhead is plural but unified. In Daniel 7, the prophet saw two divine persons; one was sitting on the throne and the other one came to him to receive an everlasting kingdom.

In the New Testament, John the Baptist encountered the other two persons of the Godhead in the baptism of Jesus. Steven saw Jesus on the right hand of the glory of God. John the apostle had a vision of the Triune God throughout the book of Revelation.

It is interesting to note that there is no detailed description of heaven in the Quran. Look for the word heaven in any Quran concordance, and you will find practically nothing about heaven. Allah boasts plenty about creating the heavens, but Mohammed saw none of it. All the Quran speaks about is paradise and gardens. The great final prophet's religion has no recorded detailed description of heaven in his book. Just read the book of Daniel and note the detailed description of heaven and contrast it with the whole of the Quran. There is not a single glimpse or sight of the throne of God in the Quran. Below are some examples outside of the context of the Bible in support of the Triune God.

I was once discussing the issue of the rejection of the Triune God in the Quran with a Turkish Muslim convert to Christ. She remarked that everything is complex in the world except Allah. Even we human beings are complex. We are also three-in-one beings (spirit, soul, and body). Muslims always complain that they can't understand the Trinity and therefore cannot believe it; yet they sit in a plane not knowing all the mechanics and mathematics involved for a plane to fly them to their destination. I wonder why they don't learn all the science involved in the constitution of a plane before flying. What is so hard about believing in the Triune God? If we Christians can believe and understand it, why is it so difficult for Muslims to believe or understand it?

The three-in-one concept is revealed in many things in nature. Romans 1 warns us that men are without excuse for not knowing the identity of the true God because the eternal power of the Godhead (The Trinity), is seen by the things that are made. For example, water exists in three forms; as liquid, vapor, and ice. Even the sun exists in three forms; heat, light, and rays. For a more detailed study of the Triune God and the scriptures relevant to it, I recommend the reader gets *God's Plan for Man* by Dakes.

Chapter 3

THE QURAN'S REJECTION OF CHRIST AS THE SON OF GOD

Next to the constant repetition of Allah having neither a partner nor an associate is Allah not having a son or Jesus not being the Son of God. The rejection of Christ's Sonship is a constant theme in the Quran and comes with the most violent condemnation possible. Sometimes, the Quran just declares that Allah has no son and at other times it mentions specifically that Jesus is not the Son of God. In both cases God is stripped of being a Father, and Jesus is stripped of being a Son. The Quran attack is a double-edged sword. It slashes God the Father and also God the Son.

4. Further, that He may warn those (also) who say, "(Allah) hath begotten a son":

5. No knowledge have they of such a thing, nor had their fathers. It is a grievous thing that issues from their mouths as a saying what they say is nothing but falsehood! (Surah 18:4-5)

They say: "(Allah) hath begotten a son": Glory be to Him.– Nay, to Him belongs all that is in the heavens and on earth: everything renders worship to Him. (Surah 2:116)
1. Say: He is Allah, the One and Only;
2. Allah, the Eternal, Absolute;
3. He begetteth not, nor is He begotten;
4. And there is none like unto Him. (Surah 112)

The Quran's rejection of Christ as the Son of God is more of an attack on the Father than the Son. It denies one of the funda-mental natures of God, that is, his Fatherhood. Let's examine an opposite passage in the Bible that directly contradict the above quranic passages and condemns it. Ephesians 1:3 says "Blessed be the God and Father of our Lord Jesus Christ, who hath blessed us with all spiritual blessings in heavenly places in Christ." The opposite of this verse could read "cursed be the god who is not the father of our Lord Jesus Christ."

If you look critically at the above verse, it is telling you that it is only the God who is the Father of our Lord Jesus Christ who is true and is blessed. There are many gods in the world; we are not necessarily speaking here about Allah. This verse cuts across any god who has no direct link with Jesus spiritu-ally and cannot therefore be Jesus' Father.

First John 2:22-23 asks the famous question, "**who is a liar?**"; then it gives you the answer. It is the one that denies that Jesus is the Christ, that is, the Savior. "He is anti Christ that denies the Father and the Son. Whoso ever denies the Son the same hath not the Father." Therefore, if the Quran denies Jesus as the Son of God, then we are warned for over

500 years before Mohammed came that he would not have the Father also and neither would those who believe on him. As you read this book I am trying my best to bring out the true conflicting messages as convincing as possible so that you will have the information and make your choice as there are too many Muslims and Christians who don't really know the serious nature of the contrast between the two religions. If all I can do through this book is to impress in your spirit that these two world-leading religions are at loggerheads, then my mission is accomplished. As to the major doctrines of the two religions there can be no compromise between the two. You cannot serve both camps. We all have to make a stand for one of them. I know there are many people on this earth who will say for peace's sake, live and let's live and not thrash out the contrasts between the religions. But unfortunately the two religious books make exclusive claims, and they both make claims on our lives. We, the human race, is caught up in these opposite and vicious claims by the two most powerful world religions, and it is important that we endeavor to at least know the exclusive claims by the two world religions so that we can make informed choices.

The whole of Psalm 2 is written against all those who would try to cut asunder the Father and the Son and would claim to be worshipping one and rejecting the other. When you read verse 2 in Psalm 2 it says all those included in this description will have a two-edged sword of attack. The first attack will be against the Father and the second attack against the Son,

Please take note that there are two "against" words in verse 2. Psalm 2 is concluded in verse 12 by giving warning to all those that claim to worship the Father without the Son and concludes with a wonderful assurance of blessings to all those that put their trust in the Son. Please take note that we are to put our trust in the Son and not in the Father. First John 1:5 says God has given us eternal life and this life is in the Son. *Eternal life was given by God the Father but is not found in him; it is found in the Son.*

Muslims enjoy the blessings and goodness of being fathers, but they hate the idea of Allah being a Father. Unfortunately, they want the blessings of being fathers but they don't want their God to have similar blessings of being a father. Listen to the conversation I had with a Muslim minicab driver few years ago.

Mr. Christian: Are you a Muslim?
Mr. Muslim: In shah Allah, meaning thanks be to Allah.
Mr. Christian: Are you a father and if not do you hope to be a father?
Mr. Muslim: Yes, I'm a father.
Mr. Christian: Is it good to have a son?
Mr. Muslim: Of course it is a good thing.
Mr. Christian: Is it a blessing to be a father and to have a son?
Mr. Muslim: Yes it is.
Mr. Christian: Is it a joy and a wonderful feeling to be a father and have a son?
Mr. Muslim: Definitely it is a joy and a privilege.
Mr. Christian: Who gave men this wonderful feeling or joy to be a father and to have son?
Mr. Muslim: It is Allah (God).

Mr. Christian: If it is Allah or God who gave men that wonderful feeling of being a father and having a son, why then does your Quran say that Allah is not a father, can never be a father, and hates to be described as being a father and certainly does not have a son. Does it mean that your Allah doesn't like good things?

Mr. Muslim: But Allah is not like men. To be a father and have a son will be to make him like men. Glory be to him; he is above having a son.

Mr. Christian: My Bible says in James 1:17 says "that all good and perfect gifts come from the Father above." You have just agreed with me that the wonderful blessings you enjoy for being a father come from Allah (God). He Allah gives you good things but hates to have the good things he gave. It doesn't make sense. Something is fundamentally wrong with your reasoning with me.

Mr. Muslim: I have told you that our Quran teaches that Allah hates being a Father and can't have a son. He's above what men impute to him.

Mr. Christian: Either Allah is the one that gave this blessedness of being a father to men or he didn't, and the Quran is lying to you Muslims.

Mr. Muslim: I have never thought about it like that, and it's the first time someone has explained it to me in this manner. I'll investigate it further.

Mr. Christian: Every day when you look at your children remind yourself that it is a blessing, joy, love, and so on to be a father and then ask yourself why Allah cannot have such blessedness. Perchance God would open your understanding for you to know the joy of believing the God who has and is a Father.

Mr. Muslim: I will try.

This conversation literally took place between me and the minicab driver. He shook my hands and drove off. If you are a Christian reader, try this with a friendly Muslim neighbor. You'll quickly observe how completely the mind of an unbeliever in Christ is completely paralyzed when it comes to spiritual issues—and I repeat, spiritual issues.

There are many passages in the Bible that express the wonderful unity, love, joy, and bond between the Father and the Son Jesus Christ our Lord. Develop a habit of reading them regularly and use them to praise the Triune God. We need some more teaching and preaching on this wonderful subject that has been hidden to the Muslims. I also pray that more songs will be written on this subject. I pray that Christians will share this light with Muslims. Some of the passages in the Bible are John 1:1-18; John 3:35, 36; John 5:17-30, 37-38 ; John 6:37-40; John 8:16-19; John 10:27-30; John 14; John 17; Matthew 12:17-21; 1 John 1:1-4; and many more.

The Muslim mind and heart desperately need to know God as a Father. One evening I was driving when a Muslim friend stopped me and asked "Why do you Christians call God your Father." I answered him, saying it's because we know him and have a relationship with him. We have been redeemed to God by the blood of his Son Jesus Christ. We have a covenant with him. We have believed his good report that he is a Father. We are spiritually bonded with him through the death and resurrection of his Son. I used the relationship between the Queen of England, the British citizens, and Prince Charles to illustrate my point. I reminded him that the subjects of U.K call the queen, Queen Elizabeth. They need special permission and to follow protocol before they can see the Queen; Prince Charles on the other hand doesn't call her Queen; he calls her mum and doesn't need any special permission or protocol to see his mum. Also the children of any national president do not call their father Mr President, they call him dad and do not need any permission to see him.

If you are a Muslim reader, please, I plead with you to reconsider your position with the Father and his son Jesus Christ. I have told you more than enough to know that truly Jesus is the Son of God. I have tried to reason with you to show you that your quranic teaching on this precious subject is wrong.

Please do not harden your heart; you know that Jesus is more than a prophet. Take a step of faith and come to the living savior. As you keep reading this book he says in Rev. 3:20, "Behold I stand at the door (your heart) and knock." Please hear his voice and open the door for him to come in.

There is a serious passage in the Quran on the Sonship of Christ that needs special reference to. It is Surah 19:88-92:

88. They say: "((Allah)) Most Gracious has begotten a son!"

89. Indeed ye have put forth a thing most monstrous!

90. At it the skies are ready to burst, the earth to split asunder, and the mountains to fall down in utter ruin,

91. That they should invoke a son for ((Allah)) Most Gracious.

92. For it is not consonant with the majesty of ((Allah)) Most Gracious that He should beget a son.

Allah says it is an abominable, monstrous, grotesque thing to say that he has a son. It goes on to say that all heaven would break into pieces, that is, the stars, moon, sun, and heaven itself and everything that is in it would be destroyed before he could have a son. Also the earth would cleave asunder; that means a total destruction of this earth. We had one mighty earthquake, and we saw a disastrous effect the resulting tsunami brought, with over 250,000 dead. Imagine an earthquake that would be so monstrous to cause the earth to split into two and all the mountains to fall down in pieces. Imagine what would happen to the world if such a thing were to happen. It would be a total destruction of the universe.

The universe has to be totally destroyed before Allah can have a son. My question for all to ponder is who alone in this wonderful universe who hates having a son so much as to destroy all the heavens, the earth, and all the mountains? I have already reasoned with you that having a son demands the greatest love, joy, and bond. Who alone in the world would so much hate to share love with another being? Is it not Satan alone who is so evil that he would never want to be father and have a son? Is it not Satan alone who would never want to share love with anyone? Is it not Satan alone who is completely autocratic and can be never challenged or reasoned with? You judge for yourself.

The book of Revelation is not mentioned at all in the Quran. I am not surprised. There is no greater condemnation of the Sonship of Christ than what is in Surah 19:88-92. I find the Quran very mocking by naming it after Mary (Surah Maryam). Since the world was founded nobody has condemned the Sonship of Christ like what is written in Surah 19:88-92, and nobody will ever write a more vicious attack than what is written there.

Mohammed, the prophet of Allah has lifted up his voice against the Holy one of Israel. He has boasted against the Lord and magnified and multiplied his words against the Lord, the Son of the living God. The children of Esau and Ishmael (Genesis 28:9) have found a channel to reinvent their ancient anger, envy, and hatred (Ezekiel 35) against the King of Zion. Like Goliath of old the vast army of Mohammed rises early and fills the airwaves with statements defying the king of Israel.

The Quran asks, "To Him is due the primal origin of the heavens and the earth: *How can He have a son when He hath no consort?* (Surah 6:101). This is the verse that ties the average Muslim's mind with the belief that for Allah to have a son he must have sex with a female, and since he finds it unthinkable for God to have sex with a female, he consequently rejects the claims of the Sonship of Christ on the assumption that it could only happen through sex. It is unthinkable for us Christians for us to imagine God having physical sex.

The sonship of Christ has nothing to do with sex. Christ existed as a son to the Father before he was incarnated in Mary's womb (Galatians 4:4). First John 1:1-3 also confirms this. Christ is the Son of God by virtue that he existed from eternity in the bosom of the Father (John1:18) and shared a glory with the Father (John 17:5). Hebrews 1 classically explains it. Many times in John 6, Christ tells us that he came down from heaven. John 6 further explains that he did not only come from heaven but was actually part of God and came out of God. The Bible is self-explanatory and very detailed. The problem is that most men are unwilling to search the pages of the Bible and find answers to their questions.

The Fatherless Christ of Islam

Listen to the following dialogue between Mr. Christian and Mr. Muslim on the Christ presented by Islam.

Mr. Christian: Do you believe that Jesus is the son of God
Mr. Muslim: I surely don't because Allah says that he does not have a son, cannot have a son and will never have a son. He is above begetting a son.
Mr. Christian: Do you believe that Joseph is the father of Jesus?
Mr. Muslim: No, I don't because the Quran says that Allah created Jesus in Mary's womb by speaking and saying "Be" and Jesus was.
Mr. Christian: So you believe that Joseph is not the father of Jesus
Mr. Muslim: That is right
Mr. Christian: Also, you believe that Allah (god) is not the Father of Jesus.
Mr. Muslim: That is right

Mr. Christian: Therefore, according to your belief and religion, Jesus is neither the Son of Allah nor the son of Joseph.

Mr. Muslim: That is right. He is always referred to in the Quran as the son of Mary.

Mr. Christian: So who is then the father of Jesus?

Mr. Muslim: I do not know. All I know is that Allah created him in Mary's womb.

Mr. Christian: What is so special about Jesus that Allah has to go to extraordinary lengths to create Jesus from nothing?

Mr. Muslim: I do not know. After all Allah can do whatever he pleases.

Mr. Christian: Therefore the Jesus in your religion is presented as a fatherless Jesus. God is not his father, and man is also not his father. Don't you think that the equation doesn't add up?

Mr. Muslim: That is what my religion teaches and I believe it.

Mr. Christian: Then your religion has many unexplained messages.

Who Is Interested in Denying Christ as Son of God?

In this big world we live in, who is interested in denying Christ as Son of God? Many people over the years have made different kinds of claims on various subjects, but the claims of Christ as the Son of God stands above every claim made by men throughout history. It is a unique claim that clearly informs the world that he is divine. If he is divine according to the claims made, then it follows to reason that he must be above every man that has ever lived, including Mohammed and all the other religious leaders who have world religions going today. Christ's claim as Son of God is the backbone of the Bible. That is why in John 8:5:17 when Jesus answered them, "My Father worketh hitherto, and I work," the Jews were mad and they knew and understood by Jesus' answer that he was claiming to be equal with God the Father.

In the baptism of Christ recorded by all the four writers of the gospels, the Father could have said so many wonderful things about Jesus, but the most specific and important thing he said is that Christ is his Son and not only his son but his "Beloved Son." We find the same statement repeated in the transfiguration story described in Matthew 17. In the baptism of Christ, immediately after the Father proclaimed Christ as his beloved Son, we find Satan coming on the scene to attack that specific accolade given to Christ as the Son of God. In two out of the three temptations Satan was specific in attaching Christ's title as the Son of God. I believe Satan was around and heard the Father proclaiming Christ as Son of God and didn't waste time in coming and confronting Jesus about that title. Listen to the tempter in Matthew 4:3, "If thou be the Son of God command these stones to be made bread." Again, in verse 6, Satan said, "If thou be the Son of God cast thyself down." Satan despised Christ's title as the Son of God with all venom. He tried to cast doubt in Jesus' mind about his role as the Son of God. Why didn't Satan attack Jesus with any other title but just with the title as Son of God? I believe this is because this title clearly proclaims and confirms his divinity which Satan hates. If Satan found it so important to attack Christ on this claim, then shouldn't we have a cause for concern if somebody else comes on the scene and makes the main focal point of his religion denying and attacking Christ's title as Son of God? I did put this question to someone, asking him what is the connection between the angel who gave the message to Mohammed and Satan since both hated the title of Christ as the Son of God.

If the angel who spoke to Mohammed and Satan both hated Christ's title as Son of God, when they could have attacked over 300 other names and titles of Christ in the Bible, then I put the same question to you, the reader, what do you think the connection is between the two angels? (Remember Satan is a fallen angel.)

There are many passages in the Old Testament that declares Christ as Son of God before Christ's advent. Here are some of them: I will declare the decree: the Lord have said to me; thou art my Son ... (Psalm 2:7); the last verse also says *"Kiss the Son."* In Isaiah 9:6 we see that the same person who is called the Almighty God existed also as a Son. When the Bible says Behold unto us "A Son is given," implies he already existed as a Son. In Proverbs 30:4, we are informed that God has a Son and asks the question: what is his name. And finally, in Psalm 72:1, King Solomon wrote that God who is a King has a Son.

The New Testament is littered with the proclamation of Christ as Son of God. The passages are too numerous to mention. Listen to a couple of scriptures by Jesus himself proclaiming to be the Son of God.

For God so loved the world, that he gave *his only begotten Son*, that whosoever believeth in him should not perish, but have everlasting life.

For *God sent not his Son* into the world to condemn the world; but that the world through him might be saved. (John 3:16-17)

[22] For the Father judgeth no man, but hath committed *all judgment unto the Son:*

[23] That all [men] should *honour the Son*, even as they honour the Father. He that honoureth not the Son honoureth not the Father which hath sent him. (John 5:22, 23)

Jesus asked the blind man he healed in John 9:35 "Does thou believe on *the Son of God*?"

One of the most ridiculous statements I constantly hear from the mouth of many Muslims and some of the unbelievers of Christ is that we are all sons of God. By this it is meant that Jesus is not different from the rest of the human race. They desperately try to blend Jesus with the rest of mankind. Each time they make such statements, I remind them that all men are sinners except Christ. Secondly, Christ's work stands above all the miracles of the prophets put together. I find in their statements an obstinate will to reject the clear evidences of Christ being the supreme Son of the living God.

Chapter 4

THE QURAN'S REJECTION OF CHRIST'S PREEXISTENCE

45. "Behold! the angels said: "O Mary! Allah giveth thee glad tidings of a Word from Him: his name will be Christ Jesus, the son of Mary, held in honour in this world and the Hereafter and of (the company of) those nearest to Allah.

46. "He shall speak to the people in childhood and in maturity. And he shall be (of the company) of the righteous."

47. She said: "O my Lord! How shall I have a son when no man hath touched me?" He said: "Even so: Allah createth what He willeth: When He hath decreed a plan, He but saith to it, 'Be,' and it is"! (Surah 3:45-47)

According to this passage in the Quran, Mary replied to angel's visitation informing her to the coming birth of her son Jesus Christ by asking how that was going to be done since she was a virgin. The angels then replied to her that

Allah will *create* Jesus in Mary's womb by just speaking and saying "Be and it is." Please note the following implication of this passage:

(a) No male seed involved in Jesus birth, thus confirming the virgin birth narration in the Bible.

(b) The conveyors of the message to Mary were *angels* while in the Bible; we are informed that there was only one angel called Gabriel who delivered the message to Mary.

(c) The word "create" was used implying that Christ did not exist before being of Mary.

(d) There was no explanation before or after this passage why Allah had to use this extraordinary way to create Jesus from nothing while there were millions of men who could have fathered Jesus. Assuming that Jesus is only a prophet as Mohammed claims in the Quran, there is no reason given why none of the great prophets like Moses and Abraham were not created like Jesus was. There was no reason given why even he, Mohammed, who was claiming to be the final prophet wasn't created like Jesus was. Surely he, being the final prophet, would have liked to be created without a male seed.

Some of the Islamic scholars are so engrossed with their fanatical hatred of Jesus to such an extent that simple statements in the Quran informing us that Jesus did not have a male seed in him being born is denied by them. They are worse than their prophet. Such an example is one Mautana M Ali. Another passage that throws light on what the Quran teaches about Christ's preexistence is found in Surah 3:59, "The similitude of Jesus before Allah is as that of Adam; He created him from dust, then said to him "be and he was" Please note the following observations.

(a) Jesus birth is likened to that of Adam.

(b) Adam was created from dust while Christ was created from nothing in Mary's womb by Allah just speaking and commanding it to be.

(c) Again in this passage, there are no reasons given by Allah why such a dramatic action. No reason is given by Allah for bypassing all the male seed available to procreate Jesus. Surely Jesus must have been very special in Allah's calculation to go such an extraordinary length to create him; but Allah, who is so desperate in the Quran to get every man to submit to his will, failed in a gigantic way to give us a single reason why he had to go through such an extraordinary length to create Jesus from nothing in Mary's womb.

Every time I ponder on this whole narration, I begin to suspect an element of deception. The additions don't add up. A friend of mine, an ardent Muslim, made me become aware of this verse of Christ's creation in the Quran in my first few months of becoming a Christian. He used to quote them both in Arabic and in English and used to tell me that I'm lost with all my Christian colleagues. The more I listened to him and the more I researched both the Quran and the Bible, the more I become convinced that it is instead he and the Muslims who are the lost ones. It is they who have been given half-baked, inconclusive, and false statements about the origin of Jesus.

Mohammed was oftentimes challenged about the truthfulness of his revelations. On this occasion, when he came out with his revelations about the creation of Jesus in verse 59, he was challenged by a Christian deputation. If you examine verses 60 and 61 carefully, you will observe that instead of giving good reasons why his revelation differed from all the prophets and all the scriptures, he treated their challenge with contempt and threatened them with a challenge to invoke a curse from Allah against who "was lying" in verse 61. He wanted the Christians to engage in what Christ had ordered them not to do in Matthew 5:33-37. Let us now examine what the Bible teaches on the preexistence of Christ. There are too many scriptures confirming the eternal nature of Christ. I will only give a handful.

For unto us a child is born, unto us a son is given: and the government shall be upon his shoulder: and his name shall be called Wonderful, Counsellor, The mighty God, The everlasting Father, The Prince of peace. (Isaiah 9:6)

In this verse, Christ is called the Mighty God who has existed from eternity. Please take note of the word **"everlasting Father,"** meaning no beginning, no ending, and always existing.

But thou, Bethlehem Ephratah, [though] thou be little among the thousands of Judah, [yet] out of thee shall he come forth unto me [that is] to be ruler in Israel; whose goings forth [have been] from of old, from everlasting. (Micah 5:2)

His origin is stated as coming from everlasting. Unfortunately the New World Translation by Jehovah Witnesses, who share the same spirit of anti-Christ as the Muslims, translated the above verse as **"Christ being created from time indefinite."** There is an eternal difference between created from time indefinite and everlasting. Anyone from everlasting can only be divine and God, while a person created from time indefinite can only be a creature and not divine.

That which was from the beginning, which we have heard, which we have seen with our eyes, which we have looked upon, and our hands have handled, of the Word of life;

(For the life was manifested, and we have seen [it], and bear witness, and shew unto you that eternal life, which was with the Father, and was manifested unto us;)

That which we have seen and heard declare we unto you, that ye also may have fellowship with us: and truly our fellowship [is] with the Father, and with his Son Jesus Christ. (1 John 1:1-3)

Christ is called here the "that eternal life" which was with the Father. Christ has always existed with the Father. Many times in the book of Revelation he describes himself as coming from eternity. He uses different phrases and words, but they all mean the same. He has always existed from eternity. Listen to him in **Revelation 1:11, "I am Alpha and Omega the first and the last."** He means here that there was no god before him and no god is coming after him. In verse 18 he further says that **"I am he that liveth and was dead."** The word **"liveth"** means no beginning or self-existing before he became man and died for our sins and now **"I am alive forever more Amen."** The eternity of Christ's origin is summarized by the scripture **"Jesus Christ the same yesterday today and forever"** (Hebrew 13:8).

John 8:12-59 is a good example of anyone who wants a proper understanding of Jesus' origin. In those passages, you can replace the Jews who were arguing with Christ with Mohammed and Muslims and you will observe that what Mohammed have written in the Quran about the origin of Jesus is not different from what the Jews in John 8 were saying. Both despised their blessed savior. Christ continuously claims in these passages that he is from above, and the rest of mankind is from below. In other words he existed before his birth by Mary. There is an interesting passage in Hebrews 10:5 which says his **"body was prepared"** beforehand.

In John 8:12-59, Jesus reminded the Jews that Abraham was glad to see him. The Jews went wild in protest and said how he could say such blasphemous words when he was not yet fifty years old. Jesus answered them with that classic statement that has baffled his enemies up to now **"before Abraham was I am."** "I am" means God and eternity. Mohammed and other religious people will say whatever they want to say about Jesus, but he still remains **"I am."**

Chapter 5

THE QURAN AND ISLAM REJECT CHRIST AS THE CREATOR AND SUSTAINER OF THE WORLD

The Quran is full of endless repetitions that Allah alone is God. Allah alone is the creator and sustainer of the universe; Allah alone is omnipotent, omnipresent, omniscient, and the originator of all things. In fact Allah hardly speaks without telling man that he alone has divine attributes and therefore all must bow, submit, and pay homage to him. Surah 112 summarizes all the above. To me his repetitive assertions borders on bragging and boasting. Apart from telling what he is, he declares that all the other gods people try to associate with him or replace him with are bogus and created nothing.

20. Those whom they invoke besides Allah create nothing and are themselves created.

21. (They are things) dead, lifeless: nor do they know when they will be raised up. (Surah 16:20-21)

In this passage Jesus' name was not directly mentioned, but from verse 20, we can conclude that it includes him because he's worshipped as God more than any other god.

2. He to whom belongs the dominion of the heavens and the earth: no son has He begotten, nor has He a partner in His dominion: it is He who created all things, and ordered them in due proportions.

3. Yet have they taken, besides him, gods that can create nothing but are themselves created; that have no control of hurt or good to themselves; nor can they control death nor life nor resurrection. (Surah 25:2-3)

We can more positively conclude that those Allah is condemning as being no god includes Jesus because his sonship claim is mentioned in verse 2. *We are told in these verses that all other gods are completely powerless. They can neither do good nor harm and do not have any control over death, life or resurrection.*

I believe these statements are misleading and far from the truth. Leaving Jesus temporarily out of the discussion, let's concentrate on all the false gods that people worship. The Bible declares that every form of idol worshipping and worshipping of false gods leads eventually to the worshiping of the devil.

But I [say], that the things which the Gentiles sacrifice, they sacrifice to devils, and not to God: and I would not that ye should have fellowship with devils.

Ye cannot drink the cup of the Lord, and the cup of devils: ye cannot be partakers of the Lord's table, and of the table of devils. (1 Corinthians 10:20-21)

It is not factually correct to say that worshipping of false gods do no harm to man. Reasoning demands that worshipping of anything false will always lead to the worshipping of Satan because he is the principal character trying to usurp God's throne. Also any worshipping of Satan will always involve the use of destructive powers. Jesus warned us of that in John 10:10, *"The thief cometh not, but to steal, and to kill, and to destroy."*

I find it hard to believe that the final prophet, the prophet of all prophets could make such a fundamental error that worshipping of false gods does not bring any harm to men. Worship of false gods ushers in serious demonization of the human race. The human race is seriously infested with demons, which is a subject completely muted in the Quran and is my topic for the next chapter. God punished Israel for worshipping false gods far more than any other sin. Worshipping of false gods opens the door for many other sins, and its effect is very destructive. Let's now examine other passages in the Quran where Jesus is specifically mentioned as not being a creator or sustainer of the world.

171. O People of the Book! Commit no excesses in your religion: Nor say of Allah aught but the truth. Christ Jesus the son of Mary was (no more than) an apostle of Allah, and His Word, which He bestowed on Mary, and a spirit proceeding from Him: so believe in Allah and His apostles. Say not "Trinity": desist: it

will be better for you: for Allah is one Allah. Glory be to Him: (far exalted is He) above having a son. To Him belong all things in the heavens and on earth. And enough is Allah as a Disposer of affairs.

172. Christ disdaineth nor to serve and worship Allah, nor do the angels, those nearest (to Allah.: those who disdain His worship and are arrogant,—He will gather them all together unto Himself to (answer)." (Surah 4:171-172)

Here Jesus is definitely rejected as the Son of God and confirmed as son of Mary and as "and only a messenger of Allah." Similar passages also talk about stripping him of his divine royalty and the role he played in creation.

75. Christ the son of Mary was no more than an apostle; many were the apostles that passed away before him. His mother was a woman of truth. They had both to eat their (daily) food. See how Allah doth make His signs clear to them; yet see in what ways they are deluded away from the truth!

76. Say: "Will ye worship, besides Allah, something which has no power either to harm or benefit you? But Allah—He it is That heareth and knoweth all things." (Surah 5:75-76)

116. "And behold! Allah will say: "O Jesus the son of Mary! Didst thou say unto men, worship me and my mother as gods in derogation of Allah.?" He will say: "Glory to Thee! never could I say what I had no right (to say). Had I said such a thing,

thou wouldst indeed have known it. Thou knowest what is in my heart, Thou I know not what is in Thine. For Thou knowest in full all that is hidden."

117. "Never said I to them aught except what Thou didst command me to say, to wit, 'worship Allah, my Lord and your Lord'; and I was a witness over them whilst I dwelt amongst them; when Thou didst take me up Thou wast the Watcher over them, and Thou art a witness to all things."

118. "If Thou dost punish them, they are Thy servant: If Thou dost forgive them, Thou art the Exalted in power, the Wise." Surah 5:116-118

Within these passages in the Quran there are serious charges and allegations leveled against Jesus, Mary, and Christians. They hint of truth mixed with gross misstatements. There are gross errors that could have easily been avoided had Mohammed taken just a little time to check the truthfulness of what he was spewing out as new and final revelations to mankind. Instead of raising an army of warriors to defend (according to Muslims scholars) his revelations, he should have spent a little of his time to investigate the matter; he would never have written what he left behind to be believed by millions. Let's examine the relevance of Mary before Jesus.

I once asked an eastern orthodox priest why their church has elevated Mary to the level of deity by calling her "the mother of God." He replied that their church gave that title to Mary in other to protect Christ's deity. He said the church knew that

Satan would introduce many false prophets and religions that would come into the world to deny and reject the deity of Christ. By calling her "the mother of God" in all their literature and liturgy throughout generations, they have established forever Christ's deity in the minds and hearts of their church adherents.

The explanation the priest gave was a little plausible, but the title could be interpreted in other ways and entirely different meanings given it. Moreover, that title was never given to Mary in the Bible. The explanation the priest gave is a classic example of men trying too hard to protect God's word. God will always protect his word. We need to stick strictly to what has been written down in the scriptures. It's interesting to note [I have repeatedly asked Roman Catholics why they worship Mary. They have all denied worshipping Mary but have said they use her as intermediary to reach Jesus] that Jesus never called Mary his "mother" in the Bible but called her "woman." For many years after I became converted I used to ponder why Jesus did that. In Matthew 12:46-50 Mary and Jesus' brethren wanted an audience with him; he turned around to the crowd and said his true brethren were those who did the will of his Father. Was Jesus being rude and nasty to his mother and brethren? The answer is definitely no.

Christ being divine and knowing what was going to happen in the church in relation to Mary gave us warning not to focus on Mary too much.

The question Roman Catholics never properly answer is that if Mary is not divine then how can she have the power to hear all their prayers and answer them? I would like to give a caution here to Muslims who might say part of Christendom have changed God's word by praying to Mary. God's word is there and remains intact. Man still remains a free moral agent and either obeys God's words or not. After all, the Muslims can also decide to go against the Quran and believe the Bible. Let's now examine what the Quran teaches about Christ's role in creation and sustaining the world since creation.

The phrase **"was only a messenger"** is repeated several times in slightly different forms in the Quran. If the Quran had said that Christ was a messenger of Allah, Christ could still have retained his divinity. After all, a messenger only carries a message. A man carrying a message for another man doesn't mean the carrier is less of a human nature. Jesus repeatedly told us in the Bible that he brought a message from the Father. Malachi 3:1 says **"Jehovah shall be a messenger of the covenant."**

It is the addition of the word *"only"* which strips Christ of his entire royal crown. That word restricts and places Christ firmly among only the human race. It denies him any claim of being involved in creating this world. The Bible definitely teaches all over its pages that Christ was directly involved in creating this world. For the above quranic passage to directly refute the Bible claims and make him only a human is of the gravest consequences. The two religions are on a head-on collision of the fiercest combat. Whoever is wrong is in serious trouble, and their adherents are in a total mess. They are bound to enter hell in untold millions.

In Surah 5:76 the Quran claims that Jesus Christ can do neither harm nor good. In other words, Christ is not capable of doing anything to man; whether to harm man or do any

74

good to man. This passage in the Quran should never be in a godly inspired book. Using the Quran's own words in Surah 19:89, the Quran here is making an abominable and monstrous assertion. It is a lie of the highest order. The heavens have to rent, earth cleave asunder, and the mountains fall down in pieces (Surah 19:90) for Jesus Christ not to do good or harm to mankind.

Why didn't Mohammed research from the Christian communities the untold good Christ did during the five-hundred-year gap between him and Christ? Why did Mohammed have to believe all that the angel told him about Jesus to be true? Couldn't that angel have been false and have brought him false messages? Didn't he have the scriptures like Galatians 1:6-9:

I marvel that ye are so soon removed from him that called you into the grace of Christ unto another gospel:

[7] Which is not another; but there be some that trouble you, and would pervert the gospel of Christ.

[8] But though we, or an angel from heaven, preach any other gospel unto you than that which we have preached unto you, let him be accursed.

[9] As we said before, so say I now again, If any man preach any other gospel unto you than that ye have received, let him be accursed.

These verses were warning him about fallen angels deceiving men to preach false message about Christ? Why was he silent in mentioning in the Quran all the miracles done by Christ disciples **in the name of Christ** long after Christ had gone to heaven as recorded in the epistles and Acts of the Apostles? Could it have been that the angel who called himself Gabriel who brought him the revelations didn't want the Muslims to read and hear of the disciples and followers of Christ doing much good to mankind in the name of Jesus long after Jesus had risen and gone to heaven? Surely I will never believe that it was lack of evidence available to Mohammed. I believe it was something more sinister than that.

Since Christ came into the world, he had never stopped doing good to mankind. The testimonies of the numerous wonderful things men have done using his name reaches the very throne of God. It has never been lack of evidence. The evidence about Christ doing good for mankind totally surrounds us and is overwhelming. If Christ is true and God is going to judge mankind on the true fullness of the gospel, then it stands to reason that God will make sure that the evidence about the gospel totally surrounds us. It is rather man exercising his stubborn will in not being willing to reconsider their desperately lost condition and examine the facts.

The good Christ has been doing in the world during our generation is in untold millions all the time. It doesn't matter what the Quran and Islam says; nothing in the world can convince the Christians in Pakistan alone that Christ does not and cannot do good to them today. They see it and experience it all the time. When they try to tell their brothers and sisters who are Muslims, they get beaten up, chased about, and told to shut up. They experience the good but are not allowed to testify about it. Instead, their fellow countrymen who are Muslims gather together in their mosques in the millions, chanting everyday that Christ can neither do harm nor good. This scenario is repeated across many nations of the world.

If you are a Muslim reader, please don't get angry with me. I don't hate or despise you because you are Muslim. We, the human race, are being taken for a ride by Satan. Satan is bent on taking many humans to hell as possible. The way he does that all the time is through giving man false beliefs. Satan will fight anybody who starts talking about the goodness of Jesus today.

Men can always read the goodness of Christ in the Bible and dismiss them with false reasoning because his deeds there were done a long time ago. It is another thing to see a blind man's eyes opened today when Christians pray for him **in the name of Jesus.** I have many videos of Christ doing marvelous things in Pakistan. Such miracles you will never find Muslims doing today in the name of Allah.

How can Surah 5:76 be true today in the nation of Nigeria? Who can convince the Christians in Nigeria today that Christ is not capable of doing good to them? Oh, how I pray to God that Muslims will challenge the truth of Surah 5:76 and investigate about the good Christ is doing in the world today. Even if one person takes up the challenge to investigate and if the person becomes enlightened about the good the Lord is doing to men today and makes a decisive shift to him, it will be worth writing this book. I pray to God that you will be such a one.

I will narrate an incident that may help illustrate my point. I once visited Accra, Ghana, to preach. I saw a Muslim displaying a big poster that said that Allah is God and Jesus is *only* a messenger from Allah. I asked him how he could justify that statement in the light of the overwhelming evidence in Ghana contrary to his statement. I said to him since I was born in Ghana I have never heard the Muslim leaders advertise and call on everyone to bring the sick to an open stadium, calling on Allah to heal the sick. But for years I have seen Christian leaders always calling on people to bring the sick and afflicted to their meetings to be prayed for in the name of Jesus. I can't say that everyone has been healed but many have been and that's why the Christian leaders keep calling. Why can't Allah who is God also give his followers, the Muslims, some power to do some of these miracles? Why only Jesus (the Messenger) is doing all the wonders? He became enraged and threatened to slap me in the face. The Christians rallied quickly to protect me and asked me to leave.

Next to the Muslim man was a mosque, I spent three days with the Muslims, sharing the gospel with them. Next to the mosque was also a church. They asked me whether all the miracles they have been hearing about in the church were genuine. I encourage them to go inside the church to check it out. They never did and constantly mocked all the miracles that were happening inside the church. This is an example of the battle that's raging around the world. Christ is constantly working wonders among his children while the skeptics never try to find out, and even when they see it, they nicely explain it away.

In Surah 5:116, we find Allah questioning Jesus why he, Jesus, asked men to worship him and Mary alongside Allah as

God. Jesus responded that he never asked men to do that and is reported as saying to men in **Surah 5:117, "Serve Allah, my Lord and your Lord."** I believe this is a direct reference to the scripture in John 20:17 when Jesus told Mary not to touch him saying **"I ascend unto my father, and your father, to my God and your God."** The quranic passage is very similar to the scripture except the word serve has replaced "I ascend unto. . . ."

A casual look at the verse may suggest that Jesus is claiming to be only a man and a servant, but a closer scrutiny will reveal that he is actually saying that he, Christ, is different from all men and he alone has a special and unique relationship with God. I have already mentioned that by the virtue of the fact that Christ from eternity dwelt in the bosom of the Father will always make him the Son of God.

Despite being told in Surah 5:76 that Christ could do neither any harm or good, there are other passages in the Quran that informs us that Christ did great wonders and miracles. They are

And (appoint him) an apostle to the Children of Israel, (with this message): "'I have come to you, with a Sign from your Lord, in that I make for you out of clay, as it were, the figure of a bird, and breathe into it, and it becomes a bird by Allah's leave: And I heal those born blind, and the lepers, and I quicken the dead, by Allah's leave; and I declare to you what ye eat, and what ye store in your houses. Surely therein is a Sign for you if ye did believe; (Surah 3:49)

Then will Allah say: "O Jesus the son of Mary! Recount My favour to thee and to thy mother. Behold! I strengthened thee with the Holy Spirit, so that thou didst speak to the people in childhood and in maturity. Behold! I taught thee the Book and Wisdom, the Law and the Gospel and behold! thou makest out of clay, as it were, the figure of a bird, by My leave, and thou breathest into it and it becometh a bird by My leave, and thou healest those born blind, and the lepers, by My leave. And behold! thou bringest forth the dead by My leave. And behold! I did restrain the Children of Israel from (violence to) thee when thou didst show them the clear Signs, and the unbelievers among them said: 'This is nothing but evident magic.' (Surah 5:110)

In this passages Christ is clearly seen doing much good to mankind. A summary is given of all the different miracles Christ performed. The phrase "by mine leave or permission" is repeated every time each act of miracle is mentioned. The intention of the inclusion of the phrase "by mine permission" was to strip Christ of any divine inherent life or power to create life and miracles. I would suggest that the inclusion of that phrase doesn't necessarily strip Christ of his divine power to create life and miracles. After all obtaining permission to do something good for mankind doesn't necessarily mean you have to be inferior to the person. It could simply mean having agreement. Christ doesn't have to be stripped of his divine royalty to obtain permission. Listen to Jesus speak directly on this subject in John 5:19,

Then answered Jesus and said unto them, Verily, verily, I say unto you, The Son can do nothing of himself, but what he seeth the Father do: for what things soever he doeth, these also doeth the Son likewise.

Note how the Jews wanted to kill him and strip him of his divine role. The very thing Mohammed is trying to do with these Surahs.

We are told continuously in the Bible that Christ had a hand in creating this wonderful world we live in and apart from creating the world, *he is the one sustaining and governing right now.* I will quote a couple of scriptures and give you a few other references. The scriptures are too many to list in this book. Note significantly the following verses:

Who is the image of the invisible God, the firstborn of every creature:

16 For by him were all things created, that are in heaven, and that are in earth, visible and invisible, whether [they be] thrones, or dominions, or principalities, or powers: all things were created by him, and for him:

17 And he is before all things, and by him all things consist.

18 And he is the head of the body, the church: who is the beginning, the firstborn from the dead; that in all [things] he might have the preeminence. (Colossians 1:15-18)

And to make all [men] see what [is] the fellowship of the mystery, which from the beginning of the world hath been hid in God, who created all things by Jesus Christ. (Ephesians 3:9)

1 In the beginning was the Word, and the Word was with God, and the Word was God.

² The same was in the beginning with God.

³ All things were made by him; and without him was not any thing made that was made. (John 1:2, 3)

He was in the world, and the world was made by him, and the world knew him not. (John 1:10)

In all the above passages we are informed clearly without any doubt that Christ was involved in creating this big world—and not only in creating but also in sustaining the world. All the miracles he performed while he was on earth and the power of attorney he had given to his disciples after his ascension were to perpetuate his sustaining of the world that he has created. He healed the blind and made the cripples walk to inform us that he created our bodies and he is very much interested in maintaining our bodies. The creator of cars makes provision to repair cars when they break down. Our creator Christ has also given us his name, his blood, his word, and the Holy Spirit to keep repairing our bodies when we break down. The expressions "by my permission" repeated in the Quran do not at all cancel his deity as many Muslims think. Christ himself said that he does not do anything outside the will of his Father because he is in perfect agreement and union with the Father. He kept also saying that the Father was testifying of him by the miracles he did that he was the only begotten Son of the Father. Note the mocking intention of the phrase "by my permission" in the Quran by Allah. What that phrase is doing is to deny that Christ has his own inherent power.

John 5:19 is a very popular verse used by Muslims to strip Christ off his deity. They always come, quoting only half that verse. They only quote part of that verse *"the Son can do nothing of himself."* They don't even humble themselves to quote the verse completely or the part of the verse that says *"that whatsoever the Son sees the Father do he the Son does likewise."* This means the Son has the power to do everything the Father does. I am amazed at the intensity and the frequency Muslims try to strip Christ off his inherent power. He said in verse 26 *"That as the Father has life in himself so has he given to the Son to have life in himself."* It is never lack of information but rather man's willful rejection of the available knowledge and information about Christ. Christ will always sustain this world as Hebrews 1:3 says *"He upholds all things by the word of his power."* Hallelujah! All things whether in heaven, earth, sea,or under the sea are sustained and upheld by the word of Christ's power. Even all those in the graves will hear the voice of the Son of God and all of them shall be raised to life (John 5:28). Please hear his voice now and live.

Mohammed tried to explain the miracles of Christ away by inferring that it had nothing to do with Christ's power,, but he never explained why Allah didn't give him Mohammed, also, that power to do the same miracles or even greater. Whom should we believe: him or Jesus?

I conclude this chapter with Hebrews 1:1-3:

[1] God, who at sundry times and in divers manners spake in time past unto the fathers by the prophets,

2 Hath in these last days spoken unto us by [his] Son, whom he hath appointed heir of all things, by whom also he made the worlds;

3 Who being the brightness of [his] glory, and the express image of his person, and upholding all things by the word of his power, when he had by himself purged our sins, sat down on the right hand of the Majesty on high;

These verses are a summary of who Christ is and what he has done in the world. He is the creator of all things and human beings (including Mohammed). He is the one that sustains or upholds all things by the word of his power. What a mighty person Christ is!

Chapter 6

THE QURAN'S REJECTION OF CHRIST HAVING POWER OVER SATAN, DEMONS, AND EVIL SPIRITS

C asting out of demons is not mentioned in any of the passages which are quoted in previous chapters where all the miracles of Christ are summarized. The Quran does not mention casting out demons by Christ. It is a phenomenon that accompanied the workings of Christ everywhere he went. How could the Quran talk about the miracles of Christ without mentioning it? I always wondered why the Quran chose not to mention it at all. What could the motive be?

Jesus asked an interesting question in Mark 3:23, *"How can Satan cast out Satan."* According to this verse, Satan will not expose himself. Satan would not like the Muslims to know that Jesus had tremendous power over Satan and demons and that he continuously expelled them from people during his preaching. Maybe by including Jesus casting out demons in the Quran, many Muslims might start investigating that phenomenon that might eventually lead them to Christ.

By excluding casting of demons from the Quran, Muslims have been denied one of the most wonderful sights one can encounter. If you, the reader, have not witnessed demons being expelled from someone before, then you are missing out on one of the most blessed experiences in life. If you were to be present to watch Christians using the name of Jesus Christ and the power invested in the blood to drive demons away from men, you life would completely change. The encounters are often so dramatic that few people that witness them and stay the same.

Human beings are infested much with demons and evil spirits:

¹And you [hath he quickened], who were dead in trespasses and sins;

² Wherein in time past ye walked according to the course of this world, according to the prince of the power of the air, the spirit that now worketh in the children of disobedience:

³ Among whom also we all had our conversation in times past in the lusts of our flesh, fulfilling the desires of the flesh and of the mind; and were by nature the children of wrath, even as others. (Ephesians 2:1-3)

According to the above passage of scripture, inclusive in the powers that control all those outside of Christ are two personalities: they are Satan (the prince of the power of the air) and demons (the spirit that now worketh in the children of disobedience). Please take note of the two words *now worketh*. They are continuous present tenses. Men without Christ are permanently under the control and influence of these two powers that hate the human soul.

All kinds of habitual sins open doors for floods of demons to invade our bodies. Driving out demons from people is one of the means that have brought revival to many countries in the past thirty years. I personally have been involved in the casting of demons in the name of Jesus for years. I have seen all kinds of demons leaving people, sometimes in dramatic ways.

About ten years ago, a friend of mine who is a minister called me after listening to my preaching tapes. He asked me why I hardly talked about yoga, knowing I preached a lot about other religions opposing the Christian faith. He and his wife told me that they have been casting out demons (called deliverance) from people, and almost everyone who had practiced yoga was infested with serpentine spirits. They testified that when they prayed for people who have practiced yoga, they often fell on the floor hissing and wriggling like snakes. They used to pray for people all day long in Leyton. They believed that yoga was far more disastrous spiritually in this nation and the western countries than Islam.

Like the snake, yoga has infiltrated the heart of this nation under the disguise of exercise. Next time you see a picture of a yogi practicing his exercise, observe and see whether you will not see the movement of a snake. Another common spirit that has possessed many people is the mermaid spirit. I have prayed for many possessed with mermaid spirits; sometimes the manifestations are similar to those who have been in yoga. The manifestations which take place when the spirits are coming out are varied and unpredictable. What we read in the Bible is almost the same thing that takes place in the world today.

Casting out demons from men in the name of Jesus is definitely one of the most important ways of recognizing that Jesus Christ is Lord and divine. When one observes how Satan and demons quake and tremble when Christ's name is invoked, it often leads people to conclude that indeed Jesus Christ is Lord. When one read scriptures like Mark 16:17, "In my name they shall cast out devils" and then sees it practiced it all over the world continuously, two thousand years after it has been spoken and recorded, we know the scriptures in Mark 16 are true. There are other scriptures like Luke 10:17-20 "Behold, I give you power to tread upon serpents and scorpions, and over all the power of the enemy" assures us of complete victory over Satan and demons.

The Quran is also silent on the abundance of miracles done by the disciples and followers of Christ after his resurrection, commission, and ascension. I believe the main reason for this silence is to deceive the Muslims. It is very easy for the Quran to explain the miracles performed by Christ away by asserting that the miracles were done expressly by the permission of Allah and not by any power inherent in Christ himself. But how could the Quran explain away *the miracles which the disciples did, using the name of Jesus?* The Quran couldn't explain it away hence went completely silent on it. Very clever isn't it?

Acts of the Apostles and the Epistles provide very detailed movements and activities of the early followers of Christ and the disciples. Their accounts and their achievements recorded in the scriptures assure us of the authenticity of the gospels. To write a religious book as popular as the Quran, which centers so much on Christ but leaves out any references to the disciples' accounts and their experiences is totally unacceptable and scandalous. We are forced to conclude that the main purpose of leaving them out is to keep Muslims in the dark about something that could be potentially of great blessing and an eye opener to them.

Muslims villages, towns and cities are littered with Malams and Imams who are desperately seeking for powers to heal the sick and cast out demons in their communities. They have been told nothing about the powers of Christ that can heal the sick and cast out demons today in Christ's name. Like the rest of mankind they are buffeted with all kinds of demonic affliction and diseases. They have been told very little about the very name that can help them in solving some of their problems. The result is that they are left in utter darkness. It is no wonder that, in every Islamic society you find amulets, charms, and Islamic leaders practicing all kinds of occultist beliefs, juju, and witch craft. Everybody in Ghana and Nigeria knows that most of the Malams are juju men.

These practices are cravings for power to solve basic and desperate human needs. I'm not saying at the moment every sickness in the Christian community is solved by Christian leaders praying in the name of the Jesus. What I am testifying is that many do get healed and delivered in Jesus' name when prayed for by Christians. As the knowledge of Christ is increasing all the time, more and more people are tending to believe Christ and the healings and deliverances are increasing all the time.

If you are a Muslim reader and you are afflicted with sicknesses and the doctors and your Malams can't cure you, seek for Doctor Jesus. When men have reached their limit, then he comes in and takes over. Listen to him calling you to come to himself in Matthew 11:28-30. Take the step of faith and go to him. If you are a Christian who is afflicted, start trusting him for your healing. Don't hang around people who believe healing and deliverance was finished with the disciples of Christ. Christ is the same yesterday, today, and forever (Hebrews 13:8). May the Lord Jesus help you and solve your problems for you.

[40]Now when the sun was setting, all they that had any sick with divers diseases brought them unto him; and he laid his hands on every one of them, and healed them.

[41] And devils also came out of many, crying out, and saying, Thou art Christ the Son of God. And he rebuking [them] suffered them not to speak: for they knew that he was Christ. (Luke 4:40-41)

Chapter 7

THE QURAN'S REJECTION OF THE JEWS AS GOD'S CHOSEN PEOPLE

I chose to include in this book the rejection of Jews as God's chosen people out of all the nations of the world because of two main reasons. First, Jesus Christ himself is a Jew, and second, he clearly said in the Bible in John 4:22 "ye (Gentiles) worship ye know not what, we (Jews) know what we worship; *for salvation is of the Jews*." How to go to God and heaven comes from the Jews and not from any other nation.

Before you start accusing God of partiality and unfairness, note that Jesus did not say that salvation is *for Jews only*. Salvation originates from them but it does not end there; it is for the whole world. It is available for everyone that believes the salvation message. The reasons why God chose the Jewish nation out of all the nations in the world, are not fully known to me. All I know is that the salvation message is available for me now. I know that God's intention towards me as my creator is good and honorable. I may not understand all his ways but I can totally depend on him to honor, love, and protect me. I don't have to hate the Jews because God chose them. If the Jews become proud and despise me because God has chosen them, God will deal with them and punish them for their sins. Let us now examine what the Quran teaches concerning the Jews. We will follow it with more details about what the Bible also says about the subject.

The Quran is full of contradictions and confusions about the role of the Jews in the affairs of God. Broadly speaking you can find surahs that:

a) Deny Jews as God's special people.

b) Accept the Jews as a special nation which has been given revealed knowledge like the Torah and Psalms which are not corrupted.

c) Assert that the Jews have corrupted the revealed knowledge given to them.

d) Say that because they (Jews) have changed God's words he has cursed them and taken away their special role from the earth as God's people.

Now let us expand on these points:

To every people (was sent) a messenger." Another translation says, "For every nation there is a message/ prophet. (Surah 10:47)

And there is not a people, without a warner having lived among them (in the past)." (Surah 35:24; another translation says prophet instead of warner.)

The Quran repeatedly teaches that prophets were raised among every nation implying that the Jews are no special people. The Quran further says in other surahs that Mohammed was given some of the prophets' names and in respect of others he didn't have their names. One of the translators of the Quran I often use, believes that because the Quran teaches that prophets were sent to all nations; it is proof that Mohammed was divinely inspired to send God's message to all the world because he alone acknowledges that all nations of the world have always had prophets. I totally disagree with him.

This claim in the Quran totally contradicts the continuous message of the Bible that all nations outside of Israel before the coming of the Savior were deeply entrenched in idol worshipping that led to the worshipping of Satan himself. King David in his thanksgiving prayer to God in 1 Chronicles 16:26 said "For all the gods of the people (Gentiles including Saudi Arabia) are idols but the LORD made the heavens." Jesus himself in commissioning Paul to take the gospel to the gentile nations said in Acts 26:17-18

Delivering thee from the people, and from the Gentiles, unto whom now I send thee, to open their eyes, and to turn them from darkness to light, and from the power of Satan unto God, that they may receive forgiveness of sins, and inheritance among them which are sanctified by faith that is in me.

The Quran assertions that prophets are in every nation is one of the main reasons why I personally find it difficult to accept Mohammed as a true prophet of the God of the Bible. His claims go completely against the facts. Idol and demon worshipping are totally prevalent in all the nations outside of Israel before the incarnation. Britain, Europe, Asia, Africa, and all islands were full of idols before they embraced Christianity.

93

There are parts of Ghana where idols are right in the center of almost every home. Even today the world outside of Christ is littered with idols. Islamic societies are not exempt from this. Lucky charms and amulets are ripe among Islamic leaders all over the world. Pictures of the black stone in Kaaba and Quran passages hang in Muslim homes, shops, offices, cars, and so forth, thinking they have magical powers to ward off evil spirits. They are all forms of idol worshipping.

It is not true that all nations have prophets; where are their writings and what are their names? Don't we find of the writings of the existing religions full of images of idols and them being worshipped? Which of the existing religions outside of the Bible talks about and gives us a solution to the human sin? Unfortunately, many Muslims, including learned men and scholars, don't take time to examine the claims of the Quran and even when they do they are fearful to contradict it.

The Jews at the time of Mohammed declared to Mohammed that they, the Jews, were God's chosen people and salvation was from them alone (Surah 2:94). Mohammed then challenged them to invoke a curse if they were truthful to their declaration to which they turned down. Let us listen to the Quran speaking in Surah 5:18 "And the Jews and the Christians say; we are the sons of Allah and his beloved ones. Say: Why does he then chastise you for your sins?" Let us also listen to scriptures in the Bible that directly contradict the above Surah.

And ye have forgotten the exhortation which speaketh unto you as children, my son, despise not thou the chastening of the Lord, nor faint when thou art rebuked of him: for whom the Lord loveth he chasteneth, and scourgeth every son whom he receiveth. If you endure chastening, God dealeth with you as with sons; for what son is he whom the father chasteneth not? But if you be without chastisement, whereof all are partakers, then are ye bastards and not sons. (Hebrews 12:5-8)

I ask you the reader which of these two writers, Mohammed or Paul, is speaking the truth and has God's word? Would you concede that Mohammed's revelation is incorrect? How can the seal of all the prophets make such a simple and fundamental mistake? Doesn't common knowledge tell us that in all homes where parents are not the natural father or mother, there are difficulties in disciplining the stepchildren and the children do not respond easily to corrections? Doesn't the scripture teach that to whom much is given much is also required from him? If they (Jews) had been given the oracles of God to bring to the rest of the world, shouldn't common sense tell us that they will carry also the brunt of God's judgments and wrath when they sin? Do not pastors and ministers of the gospel come under greater condemnation from the public when they fall into sin because they are the torch bearers of the light of Christ?

In direct contradiction to Surah 5:18 "(Both) the Jews and the Christians Say: "We are sons of Allah, and his beloved." Say: why then doth He Punish you for your sins? Nay you are but men—Of the men he created . . ." is Surah 5:20 "Remember Moses said to his people, "O my people! Call into remembrance the favour of Allah unto you, when he produced prophets among you, made you kings, and gave you what he had not given to any other among the people."

The contradiction is very clear. In Surah 5:20 the Quran is here affirming that the Jewish nation was very special to God

95

as they had a privilege that no other nation had while in Surah 5:18 the Quran is saying the opposite. On top of this I would like to point out the following:

- Apart from him Mohammed and Ishmael mentioned as prophets in the Quran, there are hardly any other prophets mentioned in the Quran who are not Jewish. The Quran is full of Jewish prophets thereby affirming that the Jewish peoples are the chosen ones.
- The Quran is full of Jewish stories from the Bible; there were no British Nigerian, or Chinese stories of history in the Quran. This also proves that the Quran affirms the Jews as special people
- There is a constant feeling of the denial of Jesus as the Son of God and also the Trinity; therefore the Quran is telling mankind that what matters most to Allah is what the Jews say he, Allah, is and not what the Europeans, Arabs, Africans, and so forth say.

I have already discussed the alleged corruption of the scripture by the Jews and so I will go on directly to the cursing of the Jews. I find the Quran very violent against the Jews. I believe it is very difficult for anyone who reads the Quran continuously to have any love, affection, or care for the Jews. I am aware that many will turn around and say to me that the Bible is also full of denouncements of the Jews.

The Bible is an historical account of the dealings of God with his people, who have been entrusted with the plan of salvation for the whole world. The Bible narrates the strength and weaknesses of the Jewish nation. The Bible tells you whatever they did whether good or bad and how God saved or punished them. Behind all the (what seems like) unending feud between God and Israel is the unfailing deep love that God has for them. Throughout the Old Testament there is a constant lamentation of the backslidings, but almost at the end of each prophet writings, there is always a promise of glorious restoration of Israel in the last days. Please read the end chapters of Daniel to Malachi in which there are unspeakable words of comfort to Israel in the last days. We find in the Quran opposite words of condemnation. The Quran pretends to be the guardian of the holy Bible and attacks and curses the Jews for corrupting the scriptures.

Listen to Allah cursing the Jews in Surah 2:65 "And well ye know those amongst you who transgressed in the matter of the Sabbath: We said to them: *"Be ye apes, despised and rejected."* The same is pronounced is made on the Jews in Surah 7:165-166. Also, in Surah 5:60 the Jews are further *cursed to be as swines.* The main contrast between Jehovah, the God of Israel, and Allah, the God of Islam, is that Jehovah punishes the Jews when they rebel but is always ready to restore them when they turn to him. In contrast to Jehovah, Allah has written them off in the Quran and has condemned them. Choose which god you would want to serve and believe.

A warning to you, the Muslim reader: be careful how you fill your heart with the hatred of Jewish people. Be careful how you hide behind the Palestinian land issue and fill your bosom with ancient hatred fuelled by the Quran against the Israelites. Be careful how you want to push all the Jews to go and live under the sea so that you can add Israel to the numerous Arab lands. Be careful to remember that the Arabs and Jews have the same father called Abraham. Try to remember how Abraham will be looking down on the Arabs from heaven of how they want to strip their cousins the Jews of the tiny piece of land given them by the Lord. Just be careful, Abraham and God are watching you with dismay from heaven.

For all the Christians who have joined the Allah band wagon, I throw out the same caution: be careful. Remember your Lord wept over Jerusalem for the plight of the Jews to follow in Matthew 23:37-39. Maybe you need to refresh your mind by reading Paul's lowliness of heart for the Jewish nation in Romans chapters 9-11. I pray to God that he softens your heart for the Israelites and all the downtrodden people of the earth.

I have already mentioned that the passages in the Quran that attack and condemns the Jews for being disobedient and tampering with the word of God far exceeds the passages that speaks of them having undiluted scriptures. Consequently, the average Muslim heart has nothing but violence against the Jews. Unfortunately this disease is not limited to Muslims. Many Christians have also fallen prey to the same lies. They don't read their Bible carefully. In fact a vast majority of the world's population are anti-Israeli because of the formation of the state of Israel. Also be careful of how you accuse me of supporting Israel blindly. It is not every action or decision the Israeli government takes I support. Sometimes I find their responses to the missile-throwing Palestinians excessive and aggressive. But I know that the problem goes much deeper than the occasional skirmishes and wars. The question that needs reflecting on is: why is it so important for the Quran to denounce the Jews and charge them of corrupting the scripture?

The answer is very simple; Jesus is a Jew, and he said salvation is of the Jews. The Bible is a Jewish book and the prophets are all Jewish. If Allah (the god of Saudi Arabia) who inspired Mohammed is not Yahweh (the God of Israel), then it is obvious that the Quran will reject the Jews as God's special people to make room for the Muslims to believe Allah's message. The Quran cannot afford to elevate the Jews to a position of special people with heavenly inspired scriptures. That will be self-destructive to its course.

Also remember that the real battle concerning the Jews is that they are the people who carried the seed of promise (the Messiah or Savior). For the Savior to be rejected, it is also critical that his roots (the Jews) be denied. Let us now reflect on few of the promises of Yahweh towards the Jews, Israel, King David, and the messiah or savior of the world.

Zechariah 8 is a wonderful chapter of the restoration of Israel in the last days when Christ comes back to rule from Jerusalem. What a glorious reign it shall be. Take note of the names Jew and Jerusalem. It will not be Saudi, Mecca, and Arab. Neither will it be Rome. London, Texas, Russia, Ghana, or China. A time will come when men will no longer flood Mecca. The last verse says

Thou says the Lord of Hosts; In those days it shall come to pass, ten men shall hold out of all languages of the nations, even shall take hold of the skirt of him that is a Jew, saying, We will go with you: for we have heard that God is with you.

Please take note of the phrase *all the languages of the nations.* That will include all the Arab and Muslim nations. Thank God for that. A time will come when the spell shall be broken and all the Hahj tour companies will cease.

Chapter 8

THE QURAN'S REJECTION OF THE DEATH AND RESURRECTION OF CHRIST

T here is total confusion in the Muslim world about what happened to Jesus from the moment he was arrested by the Jews and the Romans in the garden of Gethsemane. If you talk to a sample of 1,000 Muslims across the nations, you will have dozen of explanations of what happened to Jesus after his arrest. Broadly speaking the Muslims view of the death of Jesus can be broken into two camps:

A. The Muslims who believe that Jesus died but not for the sins of man

B. The Muslims who totally reject the death of Jesus on the cross

Both camps are riddled with fanciful stories about what happened to Jesus at the end of his life on earth. The first group is only a small proportion of Muslims, and they are mainly the Hamadiyahs. They claim that Allah played trickery on the Jews by magically printing the face of Jesus on someone else's face (they mostly say Judas Iscariot). The Jews therefore caught another person thinking that they had caught Jesus. Jesus escaped to live in India where he died a natural death at an old age. They claim that his death was neither spectacular nor sacrificial. To them all the accounts we read in the Bible after his arrest was about someone else. They don't believe the biblical account of Christ's death and totally ignore it. Some of the other scholars within this group further go on to deny clear statements in the Quran that Jesus' birth was miraculous in their fanatical hatred of anything supernatural about Christ; some of them take the fight further than their own Quran. The Hamadiyahs never support their beliefs or claims with the facts or evidence. Many times I challenged them to give the evidence in support of their claims but they just shrugged it off.

The second group of Muslims by far makes up the vast majority of the Muslim population and they consist of many factions and subdivisions. Despite having many varied opinions about what happened to Jesus after his arrest, they are all united in denying that Jesus Christ died sacrificially on the cross for the sins of mankind. They all agree that Christ was arrested in the garden but what happened after his arrest in just pure conjecture.

You will not find many Muslims united in giving you detailed accounts of what happened to Jesus after his arrest, but they all agree that Jesus was taken up by Allah and that he didn't die on the cross for our sins and therefore did not resurrect as claimed by the Bible and Christians.

Most of them claim that Allah deceived the Jews and Romans (thereby making Allah a deceiver) and took Jesus to heaven, transposing his face on Judas Iscariot or someone else. There is no clarity among the Muslims about when exactly this trickery by Allah took place. They do not tell us whether the trickery was done during the arrest in the garden or during the trial or on the cross. All they know and believe is that Allah deceived the Jews and Romans and took Jesus straight to heaven while the Jews thought they were killing Jesus on the cross. A section of Muslims actually believe that Jesus was crucified on the cross but did not die; it only appeared like death to the Jews and Romans. Mr. Ahmed Dedat, the self-styled debater of Islam versus Christianity was among this group of Muslims. He claimed during the great debate with Dr Anis Shorrock that Jesus did not die on the cross but only swooned. Let us now examine the source of this great confusion among Muslims on the arrest, crucifixion, death, and resurrection of Jesus Christ.

The source of all this confusion in Islam is the Quran. There are passages in the Quran that clearly teach that Jesus didn't die on the cross while other passages indicate that he died. Unlike the constant repetition in the Quran that Allah has no son; the passages in the Quran about the crucifixion of Jesus are not many.

DEATH	NO DEATH
Surah 3:55 Behold! Allah said "O Jesus! I will take thee and raise thee to Myself and clear thee (of the falsehoods) of those who blaspheme; I will make those who follow thee superior to those who reject faith, to the Day of Resurrection: Then shall ye all return unto me, and I will judge between you of the matters wherein ye dispute	Surah 4:157-159 157. That they said (in boast), "We killed Christ Jesus the son of Mary, the Messenger of Allah.;- but they killed him not, nor crucified him, but so it was made to appear to them, and those who differ therein are full of doubts, with no (certain) knowledge, but only conjecture to follow, for of a surety they killed him not:- 158. Nay, Allah raised him up unto Himself; and Allah is Exalted in Power, Wise;- 159. And there is none of the People of the Book but must believe in him before his death; and on the Day of Judgment he will be a witness against them;-
Surah 19:33 33. "So peace is on me the day I was born, the day that I die, and the day that I shall be raised up to life (again)"! Surah 5:117 117. "Never said I to them aught except what Thou didst command me to say, to wit, 'worship Allah, my Lord and your Lord'; and I was a witness over them whilst I dwelt amongst them; when Thou didst take me up Thou wast the Watcher over them, and Thou art a witness to all things.	

The Quran passages on the left teach the death of Jesus with lack of clarity while the passages on the right teach unequivocally that Jesus did not die. This discrepancy has been the despair of many Muslim commentators. The Islamic scholars and their commentators can't agree on exactly what happened to Jesus after his arrest in the garden, and consequently the average Muslim is also confused. I will narrate how I was introduced to this hot dispute between Christians and Muslims concerning the death of Jesus.

My colleague who was a Muslim when I became a Christian, whom I have already mentioned, challenged me to prove to him from the Old Testament scriptures that Jesus was crucified and died on the cross. This was literally during the first few months of my conversion to Christ, and I at that time didn't know the scriptures especially the Old Testament. He used to affirm that the Christians are blaspheming by saying that that Jesus was crucified and died on the cross. He often asked "How could God allow such a noble prophet like Jesus to be killed by the hands of the Romans and Jews?" Often when he made such statements he totally ignored the numerous prophets which were killed in the Bible for preaching. He never remembered that even John the Baptist lost his head for preaching. My colleague never asked himself: how can God allow John the Baptist' head to be cut off?

Sometimes he actually went further by claiming that the New Testament didn't support the crucifixion and death of Jesus on the cross. One of the passages he used to try and confuse me in believing that Jesus did not die on the cross is Hebrews 5:7 "How in the days of his flesh, when he had offered up prayers and supplications with strong crying and tears unto him that was able to save him from death, and was heard in that he feared;" He knew this scripture and quoted it often. To him this scripture supported his belief and the Quran passage in Surah 4:157-159.

If one reads Hebrews 5:7 in isolation, it may seem to support the surah but when read in context of the whole chapter it becomes clear that it refers to Christ being delivered from the powers of death to be resurrected. The chapter is not teaching that he didn't die at all like my friend was trying to convince me. Verse 8 of Hebrews 5 declares that Jesus was the only son, and verse 9 talks about him being the author of eternal salvation; both claims are inherently denied by Islam and my colleague.

I found my friend's continuous effort in trying to prove to me that the New Testament doesn't teach the death of Jesus on the cross to be the most ridiculous and self-deceptive thing ever. It is bad enough to try to claim that the Old Testament doesn't teach the death of Jesus on the cross, but to assert that the New Testament doesn't teach the death of Jesus of Christ is obstinate blindness. How can the New Testament exist without the death of Jesus on the cross? Below are a few scriptures from the Old Testament, prophesying the crucifixion and death of Jesus Christ long before it happened:

A. Psalm 22—this Psalm is a summary that has happened before his arrest in the garden. It is broadly divided into four sections:

    a. Arrest in the garden of Gethsemane and the sufferings during his crucifixion (verses 1-11)

b. His death on the cross (verses 12-18) Verse 15 says *"My strength is dried up like a potsherd; and my tongue cleaveth to my jaws; and thou has brought me into the dust of death."*

c. His victory over death (verse 19-21)

d. His resurrection and the joy it will bring on to the world

B. Isaiah 53—this chapter is a mirror of the arrest, trial, imprisonment, crucifixion, death and resurrection of Christ. Several phrases are used to inform us of his death. *"He is brought as a lamb to the slaughter (verse 7). He is cut out of the land of the living (verse 8). He made his grave with the wicked and the rich in his death (verse 9)."* He has poured out his soul unto death *(verse 12)."*

C. Daniel 9:24-27—part of this passage says *"that after threescore and two weeks shall the Messiah's be cut off but not for himself (verse 26)"*. Other translations of the same verse used the word "killed" instead of cut off.

Later on in my Christian walk when I found out about the scriptures and others informing us that the Messiah would die for our sins, I tried many times unsuccessfully to get my Muslim colleague to go and read the above scriptures. He flatly refused. Not one time did he humble himself to examine the scriptures.

Let us now examine what the New Testament teaches concerning the death of Christ on the cross. The best person to ask is the Lord himself; the One who went through it is the best person to inform us. Jesus continuously announced his impending crucifixion and death before it happened. The passages are too numerous to quote in this book. Using the book of Matthew, I will quote only a few of the passages and give other references for further reading: Matthew 12:40; 16:21-23; 17:9, 22, 23; 20:17-19; 21:33-39; 26.

A good chapter to read to get a proper understanding of the death and resurrection of Jesus Christ is Matthew 26. The whole chapter was about the impending crucifixion and death. Take note of how many times his forthcoming death, burial, and resurrection are mentioned.

The rest of the New Testament is full of numerous references to the death and resurrection of Jesus Christ. These references inform us of the death and resurrection of Jesus and go further to explain the spiritual importance of his death and the numerous benefits it brings to man. I had many questions which troubled my mind during my first year of conversion regarding the full ongoing war between what the Muslims believe on Christ's death and resurrection and what the Christians believed. In particular, why Allah, Islam, Mohammed, and the Quran should be interested in telling the Muslim that Jesus did not die on the cross?

The seriousness and consequences of Muslims' rejecting the death and resurrection of Jesus can only be fathomed by having a proper knowledge of what the Bible says about the topic. The more one learns about the topic in the Bible, the more the person feels powerless and bewildered that Islam rejects the death and resurrection of Jesus. Recently, a pastor friend showed his frustration on the subject during a seminar I was holding on the subject. He said from the day he learned that the Muslims rejected the death and resurrection of Christ he was astonished. Most of his frustration was heaped on the Christian community and their leaders for saying and doing very little on the subject. This next chapter will illustrate and enlighten us on the dire consequences of Muslims rejecting the death and resurrection of Jesus Christ.

Having shown and confirmed that both testaments teach the death of Christ let us now find out why it was necessary for someone to die for our sins and, second, why that person had to be Christ.

The first point is based on the scripture Romans 6:23 that says the wages of sin is death. Let us critically reflect on this scripture.

Any honest man will admit that he has lied and sinned before. Because we have all sinned, we all deserve a wage from God; that is death. That death means death to the flesh and death to the soul and spirit. We see the evidence of death to the flesh everyday—each time we see the hearse passing. Such incidence is a constant reminder of Romans 6:23. Death to the soul is unseen physically, but it happens. It means eternal separation of the soul and the eternal punishment of the soul because the soul according to the Bible is ever living and can never be destroyed (Genesis 2:7). See the reference from *Dake's Reference Bible Commentary* on Romans 6:23 "Divine justice is under obligation to give sinners their wages or be in debt to them forever." Since God will not owe any man forever, it is logical that God has to come up with a solution and that solution is the death of someone. Christ offered himself to the Father to die substitutionally for us. See 2 Corinthians 5:21.

Second, below are the reasons that person could only be Jesus and no one else:

A: That person had to be a human being.

B: That person had to be divine.

C: That person had to be sinless.

D: That person's blood had to be involved.

We will now look at these points in turn.

That person had to be a human being.

According to Romans 5 from verse 12, disobedience, offense, judgment, condemnation, sin, and death came into the world by one man, Adam; therefore, the opposite can only come into the world by another man. This requires that someone who is obedient, pleasing to his father, righteous, holy, and wholly blameless. Christ is the only person who falls into this description. It is interesting to note that there is no passage in the Koran that refers to Jesus being sinful, while Mohammed was instructed to ask for forgiveness of sins.

That person had to be divine.

Because sin numerically is infinite, the person who could die for our sins also must be infinite. For instance the number of lies that goes to the nostrils of God in one day amounts to innumerable millions and millions. By the time you add up all the lies from Adam up to now, it is so huge in the nostrils of God that it is beyond comprehension. This person who is qualified to die for the sins of the world must have infinite power, infinite legal authority, and infinite scope to be able to pay for all the sins of mankind. The Bible clearly teaches that Christ is divine. *"Without controversy great is the mystery of godliness; God was manifest in the flesh" (1 Timothy 3:16).*

It is only a divine person who can be infinite and be able to cope.

That person had to be sinless.

No one can die for the sins of the world if he himself is sinful. We are told repeatedly in the Bible that the Messiah or the Savior is sinless. See Isaiah 53:9 and Daniel 9:24, 27.

That person's blood had to be involved.

Let us refer to the Leviticus 17:11 "For the life of the flesh is in the blood: and I have given it to the altar to make atonement for your souls; for it is the blood that maketh atonement for the soul."

"Without the shedding of blood there is no remission of sins," the scripture says in Hebrew 9:22. Our life is in our blood. Therefore, someone had to die because we have sinned. This person who would substitute himself for our sins had to sacrifice his blood to give his life for our sins. This is why the Bible teaches a lot about the relevance of Christ's blood for our redemption. Revelation 1:5 says *"For unto him that has loved us and washed us from our sins in his own blood."*

It is only the blood of Christ that can wash us from our sins because his blood is holy. His blood came direct from God the

Father. It did not come through the instruments of man. It has been proven scientifically that the blood of a child comes from the father.

It is interesting to note that the Quran confirms that Jesus did not have a biological father. However, the Quran fails to inform us why only Jesus came to earth without a father. The Quran gives only a half-baked story while the Bible explains all its main doctrines. The blood of Jesus Christ did not overcome death alone but overcame the works of Satan and demons as well. I've seen it myself where the blood of Jesus has been invoked and the person being prayed for who is possessed by demons screams out.

To the Muslim reader, I plead with you to consider that you have been given bits and pieces of information in the Quran and that you have not been given the whole complete picture. Please go to the true and original source, which is the Bible and read it. All the knowledge of Jesus dying for us is detailed in the Bible. Jesus truly died on the cross for our sins. He has already done it. All he requires from us is to accept and believe.

The Significance and Benefits of Christ's Death for Both God and Man

I have already mentioned that without the death of Christ, God would be indebted to man forever to pay them their eternal wages, which is death. Another benefit to God from this perspective is that the death of his Son will silence all foes who at the Day of Judgment may try to prove the unfairness and injustice of God. Presumptuous men including Satan may attempt to accuse God that he is not willing to taste the heavy burden of death and yet impose death on men. No one will be justified in attacking God of this injustice when his own Son had subjected himself to death. Also, there is the issue of God's wrath being fulfilled and pacified.

From man's viewpoint, following are some of the blessings of Christ's death to the human race. From the days of Adam and Eve until today, men have always been fearful of death throughout all their lifetimes. Men have always known that death will surely come one day, but men have been totally left in the dark about when it will come and in what manner and form. Men do not know if it will be with intense suffering or not. This cloud of uncertainty has always bewildered man and held them in total fear and bondage. **Hebrews 2:14, 15 says**

Forasmuch then as the children are partakers of flesh and blood, he also himself likewise took part of the same; that through death he might destroy him that had the power of death, that is, the devil;

And deliver them who through fear of death were
all their lifetime subject to bondage.

We are told that death had a nasty sting which is sin. Since Christ was sinless and fulfilled the law, he has removed this nasty sting. "O death, where is thy sting? O grave, where is thy victory? The sting of death is sin; and the strength of sin is the law" (1 Corinthians 15:55, 56). Another important blessing derived from Christ's death is stated in Hebrews 2:14 which says "that through death, he might destroy him that had the power of death, that is, the devil."

Of all the arsenals under Satan's belt, death is his chief weapon and the nastiest of them all. Death is a summary of everything that is evil. Christ by dying for us has disarmed Satan of his deadliest weapon. That is why Jesus said in Revelation 1:18 that it is he who has the keys to hell and death. What a wonderful blessing to have the founder of your religion possessing the keys to the two of the most dreaded places in the world. Many times when we Christians remind our Muslim brothers, they get angry and accuse us of arrogance and presumption.

We do not share our testimonies about Christ to embarrass or make the Muslim angry. We do it so that they, the Muslims, will know and learn that there is a way out of the human mess and that way is sustained by a living hope and power. Let us now examine the implications of the biblical assertions that Christ resurrected from the grave.

The Significance and Benefits of Christ's Resurrection

What good is death without resurrection? What will it benefit the human race if Christ were to die for our sins but did not resurrect? What evidence do the Christians have to prove to Muslims that their message and belief about Jesus is the truth if their leader remained dead in the grave like Mohammed— even if he claimed to die for the sins of the world.

Death and the grave have closed their prison doors and shut up the human race from the day of Adam up to now. Many religious leaders have come and gone, and they have all been shut up in the grave. Their bodies lie rotten in the tombs. Many great men, kings, conquerors, and empire builders have come and gone. The grave has thick prison doors and bars; once you go there you are doomed.

From the day Adam was created, can you count how many bodies the grave has locked up and damned? Can you count how many would have loved to escape those unstoppable prison doors? Just imagine the billions of men since Adam that have been shut up in this vast prison. Could they fill the Atlantic Ocean or the Pacific Ocean? Imagine a vast ocean filled with dead people. Everyone would have loved to be revived and stand upright, but none can.

Imagine out of that vast ocean of dead people, one claiming to be the Son of God, and challenging the people, Satan, sin, and death, saying "Destroy this temple and in three days I will raise it up.... But he spake of the temple of this body" (John 2:19, 21). Suddenly out of this vast ocean of dead people, one is reminded of this great power and authority over death and the grave. He reminded himself at what he told his disciple when he was alive with them.

Therefore doth my Father love me, because I lay down my life, that I might take it again. No man taketh it from me, but I lay it down of myself; I have power to lay it down; and I have the power to take it again. This commandment have I received of my Father." (John 10:17-18)

He began to shake death's chains away. The glory of the Father filled the tomb to melt away the death chains (Romans 6:4). The Holy Spirit also got involved (Romans 8:11). The angels also got involved. An angel came from heaven and rolled the stone away. The Hallelujah choruses started in heaven. The foundations of hell shook violently. Satan and his cohorts couldn't believe their eyes! They thought they had forever captured the Lord of Glory.

Can you imagine the rapture in heaven as he shook himself from the clutches of hell and the grave? Going back to the image of the vast ocean of the dead, can you imagine him rising up from this vast ocean? Can you imagine one rock rising up from the ocean bed until it becomes a huge rock in the middle of the vast ocean?

The angels started the great hymn "My hope is built on nothing else, but Jesus Christ and his righteousness." Christ grabbed the keys to death and Hades and descended to paradise. He took the souls of the saints who were to have gone to heaven but couldn't go. He joined their souls to their bodies, put life into them, opened their graves, and took them to heaven. They had a stopover to visit their loved ones, waved them goodbye, and ascended into heaven Matthew 27:51-52.

For forty days, Christ began to show himself to the disciples that he was alive. Read the account of Paul the Apostle in 1 Corinthians 15.

The Need for Christ to Reveal Himself

Imagine Christ resurrected from the dead but did not show himself physically to his disciples and his followers. Supposing he just resurrected and went straight to heaven without showing himself physically to his disciples? There would have been

115

lingering and perpetual doubts in the mind and hearts of the disciples throughout their lives. There is a real possibility that the disciples would have had this lingering doubt as to what truly happened to Jesus' body. For such an important message like the gospel, it was critical that Jesus had a solid foundation based on facts and evidence. He couldn't afford to ascend to heaven without giving his disciples and his followers hard evidence which the Bible refers to as "infallible proof" of his physical resurrection from the dead.

The Bible clearly states in Acts 10:41 that God chose beforehand the people Christ was to reveal himself to after his resurrection. This aspect of Christ's resurrection should never be underestimated. If you are a Christian reader, I suggest that you constantly proclaim and affirm the post-resurrection appearances to the disciples in all your teaching and preaching, especially to the Muslims.

The Muslims have been told in the Quran that Allah took Jesus straight to heaven. The physical appearances of Christ in is resurrected body totally disclaims the message of the Quran that Allah took him to heaven without death and resurrection. If you are a Muslim reader, I pray to God that you carefully read those passages in the Bible. They are mostly found in the last two chapters of each of the four gospels. They contain too many detailed accounts for it not to be true.

I plead with you that when you compare and contrast the account in the gospels and 1 Corinthians 15, to the casual description of what happened to Jesus after his arrest in the Quran, you will see that one is bound to conclude that the biblical account is precise and detailed about what happened, while the quranic account is pure conjecture. If you, the Muslim reader who is sincerely seeking for truth, take the time and effort to contrast the two accounts in the two books, I believe that God will reveal to you which account is true. Long after the ascension of Christ, the disciples continued to testify in the rest of the Bible that they saw the resurrected Christ. Christ's resurrection was featured in all their preaching. One of the most famous accounts is that of doubting Thomas, which both Christians and Muslims alike know. At one occasion, Jesus appeared to the disciples without Thomas and later on when they informed Thomas that they had seen the risen Christ, Thomas said he would not believe unless he could see where they had nailed his hands and pierced his side. The Bible says on another occasion later a few days later, that the Lord again appeared to the disciples and that on this occasion Thomas was with them. He went straight over to Thomas and said to him in John 20:27-29

Then saith he to Thomas, Reach hither thy finger, and behold my hands; and reach hither thy hand, and thrust [it] into my side: and be not faithless, but believing.

28 And Thomas answered and said unto him, My Lord and my God.

29 Jesus saith unto him, Thomas, because thou hast seen me, thou hast believed: blessed are they that have not seen, and yet have believed.

I recall an incident which took place a long time ago. I read the above passage of scripture to a Muslim guy at Speaker's Corner in Hyde Park, London. He shouted out in response to my reading that Thomas had seen Jesus and therefore believed, but that he hadn't seen him and still did not believe.

Now the question is, do you believe? To you the reader, Jesus said to Thomas, "Thomas because you have seen me, you believe *but blessed are those who have not seen me and yet believe."*

Dear reader, I plead with you to please believe that Christ rose from the dead. The evidence about his resurrection and his appearance to his followers is overwhelming. Believe in the Jesus who died and rose again and not in the Jesus who never died and rose again from death as described in the Quran. The quranic Jesus who did not die and therefore was not resurrected can do nothing for your soul. The Jesus of the Quran never paid for your sins, never overcame death and the grave, and never resurrected. *The Jesus of the Quran, that is, the "another Jesus" which the Quran preaches is worthless* (see 2 Corinthians 11:3, 4) because man is not able to receive eternal life or blessings from him. Why bother about a message that cannot do anything for you spiritually? What good is it to mankind for the Quran to record that Allah took Jesus straight to heaven without death and resurrection? In fact I even dare to say that the so-called final revelation from God should not even contain that message about Jesus when it serves no real purpose or benefit for the human race. If you believe Allah took Jesus straight to heaven without death and resurrection, what are you going to benefit from him? Nothing! The Quran does not record that man will receive a single benefit from God by believing its message.

We now turn our attention to the result and the effect of Christ's appearance to the disciples after his resurrection. There was an immediate and dramatic change of heart and conviction that Christ resurrection brought to the disciples and the world. The post-resurrection appearances of Christ dramatically strengthened the conviction of the disciples about Christ's deity and that he is the supreme commander of the universe. Among the disciples, those who had any form of doubt throughout his earthly ministry suddenly were transformed beyond comprehension. A new spirit and boldness came over them. Instead of Peter swearing and cursing that he did not know Jesus, he was filled with boldness, not fearing for his life and proclaiming the gospel fearlessly with the rest of the disciples. They quickly filled the whole of Judea, Jerusalem, and Israel with the gospel.

From that moment Jesus resurrected, the disciples clearly understood Jesus' words in John 12:24, No one can multiply unless he first dies himself. Jesus couldn't multiply and bear much fruit unless he first died himself. Resurrection comes only after death, and it comes with multiplication.

After his resurrection, Christ was multiplied into his disciples by his Spirit. Instead of one person, Christ became many. He used the hands, feet, and mouths of the disciples to multiply himself. Praise is to God. There is no village or town anywhere in the world today where his name is not known or has not been honored. Today he is worshipped as the Lord for reigning supreme in this earth because of his resurrection from the dead. Let us never forget the resurrection of Jesus Christ from the grave. I pray that God empowers us to proclaim the gospel fearlessly throughout the earth.

The grave of Jesus became empty. It has been empty ever since. The bones of every person who has died can be traced today. No one has ever produced the body of Jesus because he was resurrected from the grave. Listen to him speaking in Revelation 1:18, "I [am] he that liveth, and was dead; and, behold, I am alive for evermore, Amen; and have the keys of hell and of death."

Chapter 9

THE QURAN'S REJECTION OF CHRIST'S SACRIFICIAL ATONEMENT

Surah 22:37	Leviticus 17:11
It is not their meant nor their blood, that reaches God: it is your piety that reaches Him: He has thus made them subject to you, that you may glorify God for His Guidance to you and proclaim the good news to all who do right	For the life of the flesh is in the blood: and I have given it you upon the altar to make atonement for your souls: for it is the blood that maketh atonement for the soul. **Hebrews 9:19-22** For when Moses had spoken every precept to all the people according to the law, he took the blood of calves and of goats, with water, and scarlet wool, and hyssop, and sprinkled both the book, and all the people. Saying, This is the blood of the testament which God hath enjoined unto you. Moreover he sprinkled with blood both the tabernacle, and all the vessels of the ministry. And almost all things are by the law purged with blood; and without shedding of blood is no remission.

The Quran says it is neither the meat nor the blood of animals that reaches Allah. The above passage of scriptures says **"it is the blood that maketh atonement for the soul" and "without shedding of blood there is no remission."** Who is speaking this great lie? Is it the Quran or the Bible? Is it Mohammed or Moses? Is it Mohammed or Paul? Moses and Paul, the prophets of Jehovah, the God of the Bible, are saying that God will not forgive the sins of men without blood sacrifice while Mohammed the prophet of Allah says the blood or animal is not what Allah wants but the piety of Muslims.

Surely whoever is speaking this great lie must be inspired only by Satan! It is impossible for these three great human personalities whose writings have so much dominated the human race to come from the same God, be all true prophets of God, and write such opposing scriptures with Moses and Paul on one side and Mohammed on the other side.

In one of my old Bibles, I underlined with red ink all the Old Testament passages where blood sacrifices were referred to. My Bible became littered with red coloring throughout. Without blood sacrifices there is no Old Testament and no worshipping of God. To you the reader who has read the Old Testament, I would like to ask you, how could the whole Old Testament be possible to read without the sacrifice of animals? How could we sincerely accept Mohammed as a prophet of the God of Israel when the religion he introduced into the world denies such a fundamental issue? Don't we have cause to be alarmed? When Muslims keep saying to us that they believe and worship the same God as the Christians and Jews, don't we have good reason to question why their religion denies something that is central and cardinal in our religions? If you are a Muslim reader and you retort that we have changed God's word, I would ask you to show us when all the Jews and the Christians held a world conference to change the Old Testament because the two groups are holding the same Old Testament today.

If Jehovah, the God of Israel, is the only true God and he told Moses and all the prophets of Israel that he neither forgives and cannot forgive anyone's sin without blood sacrifices, then it stands to reason that anyone who doesn't believe or deny his warning will still bear his sins. The presence of sins makes us unclean and guilty. I have always wondered since I understood this spiritual topic whether when the Muslims are told to wash their faces, hands and feet before prayers, it is because they might be feeling spiritually unclean.

A Muslim friend once alleged that we Christians don't wash our hands and feet before praying, and therefore we actually come before God unclean. I asked him if the Muslims by washing their hands and feet makes them clean and by the same token shouldn't the Christian by taking a shower or having a bath before going to church, also make them clean? He declined to answer. Moreover, it is not only in church that we pray. More importantly, human sin is not in our hands, feet, and so forth. It is in our heart and blood. Sin is a spiritual issue emanating from the heart which is kept alive by blood.

Because Islam rejects blood sacrifice as essential to the worshipping of Allah, it is easy and natural to reject the whole concept of Jesus shedding his blood on the cross for our sins. If Allah doesn't need the blood of animals to be worshipped, certainly he wouldn't need the blood of Jesus before being worshipped since the Bible clearly teaches that the blood of Christ on the cross is an extension and final sacrifice to appease God for our sins.

Listen to Christ speaking in Matthew 26:28, "For this is my blood of the New Testament, which is shed for many for the remission of sins." Surely, one of the two, Jesus or Mohammed, is telling a lie. The presence of sin is the only thing that will damn our soul and deny us access to God.

Please read all the different types of sacrifices and offerings which God commanded Moses and Aaron in the book of Leviticus, chapters 1-10. In these chapters God commanded Moses and Aaron to perform many offerings and sacrifices based on meat and blood. In Leviticus 9:24, the Bible said after they had performed all the sacrifices and offerings and blessed the people of Israel, the glory of the Lord appeared unto all the people and there came a fire out from the Lord that consumed the burnt offering and the fat upon the altar. When all the people saw this they shouted and fell on their faces. God (Yahweh) was very much interested in these sacrifices and the offerings of meat and blood.

Allah is not interested in meat and blood sacrifices for the sins of the people but Yahweh was during the reign of Aaron and his sons. Can you imagine Aaron and all his sons, the Levites and the Priests as described in the Torah, without sacrifices? Without the sacrifices of animals there would be no Torah at all. Also note that all these sacrifices are chronicled and documented in the history of Israel and can be verified outside the Bible recordings even to this day. Many of these sacrifices are still being performed and upheld today by Jews who have rejected the final sacrifice of Christ on the cross. Let us now look at some examples in the Bible where the sacrifices of animals took place.

King David

King David tried to number the people for war when God had not told him to go to war. God was very displeased with him and sent the Prophet Gad to give him three options in relation to what his punishment should be. The story is found in 2 Samuel 24. God sent an angel to slay the people of Israel. Gad the Seer went and told David in order to appease him he must raise an altar unto God and make sacrifices unto him. The last verse in Chapter 24 says "²⁵And David built there an altar unto the LORD, and offered burnt offerings and peace offerings. So the LORD was intreated for the land, and the plague was stayed from Israel."

In the time of King David, Yahweh was very much interested in meat and blood sacrifices. The sacrifice had a dramatic effect on Yahweh, and he stopped the plague. Clearly the Allah who spoke to Mohammed is not the Yahweh who sent the plague to Israel.

King Solomon

Another interesting story was that of Solomon when he built the temple. During the dedication of the temple, the Bible says in 1 Kings 8:63,

And Solomon offered a sacrifice of peace offerings, which he offered unto the LORD, two and twenty thousand oxen, and an hundred and twenty thousand sheep. So the king and all the children of Israel dedicated the house of the LORD.

Just think of the number of animals he sacrificed and the amount of blood spilled to appease God and for God to accept his prayers. The Bible says that the glory of the Lord filled the temple. God smelled the sweet fragrance of the sacrifices, and his glory came to settle on the temple. The true glory of God has not changed one little bit. He is the same yesterday, today, and forever. He has made a law from the beginning that it is the blood that makes atonement for soul. Nothing has changed and nothing will ever change. Clearly the God that Solomon worshipped and sacrificed to is not Allah, and Allah is not Solomon's God. Choose this day which of these two deities, God or Allah, you want to believe in.

Finally, let us look at the famous Lord's Supper popularly known as The Communion by comparing Jesus' words in **Matthew 26:26-29** as opposed to Mohammed's verses in Surah 22:37. Matthew 26: 26-29 says,

26And as they were eating, Jesus took bread, and blessed it, and brake it, and gave it to the disciples, and said, Take, eat; this is my body.

27 And he took the cup, and gave thanks, and gave it to them, saying, Drink ye all of it;

28 For this is my blood of the new testament, which is shed for many for the remission of sins.

29 But I say unto you, I will not drink henceforth of this fruit of the vine, until that day when I drink it new with you in my Father's kingdom.

Christ says he shed his blood for many for the remission of sins. Allah is not interested in any form of blood sacrifice. Therefore I can only conclude that the God who is the Father of Jesus, the God who is interested in the blood of Jesus, is not Allah. The God who spoke to Mohammed has no interest whatsoever in the blood sacrifice of animals. Please make a choice in which God to believe in and in choosing be wise. If all the Bible prophets said Yahweh demanded blood and the Mohammed says no, Allah does not require blood then Mohammed is not among Yahweh's prophets. He was the prophet of another god.

Sometimes when I point out this fact to Muslims they say I am wrong because they do sacrifice during Eid. I know I am not wrong because if then one asks them whether those sacrifices will make any difference to the issue of their sin, they will reply no. They kill those animals for feasting, not for forgiveness of sin. Muslims have no knowledge or understanding of atonement for sins through blood sacrifices. In fact they reject the whole concept. It is foolishness to them. "The preaching of the cross (Jesus' sacrifice) is to them that perish foolishness; but unto us which are saved it is the power of God," the scripture says in 1 Corinthians 1:18.

The most detailed teaching in the Bible about the sacrifice of Jesus is found in John 6. Please read the chapter many times over and study it. I conclude the chapter with the precious words of Jesus in verses 51-58

I am the living bread which came down from heaven: if any man eat of this bread, he shall live for ever: and the bread that I will give is my flesh, which I will give for the life of the world.

[52] The Jews therefore strove among themselves, saying, How can this man give us *his* flesh to eat?

[53] Then Jesus said unto them, Verily, verily, I say unto you, Except ye eat the flesh of the Son of man, and drink his blood, ye have no life in you.

[54] Whoso eateth my flesh, and drinketh my blood, hath eternal life; and I will raise him up at the last day.

[55] For my flesh is meat indeed, and my blood is drink indeed.

[56] He that eateth my flesh, and drinketh my blood, dwelleth in me, and I in him.

[57] As the living Father hath sent me, and I live by the Father: so he that eateth me, even he shall live by me.

[58] This is that bread which came down from heaven: not as your fathers did eat manna, and are dead: he that eateth of this bread shall live for ever.

Sacrifice! Sacrifice!! Sacrifice!!! That is the message of the whole Bible. Without it there is no Bible at all. Please read Hebrew 10 many times and join me in reading these verses 1-14 aloud

For the law having a shadow of good things to come, *and* not the very image of the things, can never with those sacrifices which they offered year by year continually make the comers thereunto perfect.

2 For then would they not have ceased to be offered? because that the worshippers once purged should have had no more conscience of sins.

3 But in those *sacrifices there is* a remembrance again *made* of sins every year.

4 For *it is* not possible that the blood of bulls and of goats should take away sins.

5 Wherefore when he cometh into the world, he saith, Sacrifice and offering thou wouldest not, but a body hast thou prepared me:

6 In burnt offerings and *sacrifices* for sin thou hast had no pleasure.

7 Then said I, Lo, I come (in the volume of the book it is written of me,) to do thy will, O God.

[8] Above when he said, Sacrifice and offering and burnt offerings and *offering* for sin thou wouldest not, neither hadst pleasure *therein;* which are offered by the law;

[9] Then said he, Lo, I come to do thy will, O God. He taketh away the first, that he may establish the second.

[10] By the which will we are sanctified through *the offering of the body of Jesus Christ once* for all.

[11] And every priest standeth daily ministering and offering oftentimes the same sacrifices, which can never take away sins:

[12] But this man, after *he had offered one sacrifice for sins for ever*, sat down on the right hand of God;

[13] From henceforth expecting till his enemies be made his footstool.

[14] <u>For by one offering he hath perfected for ever them that are sanctified.</u> Halleluyah!

Chapter 10

THE QURAN'S REJECTION OF CHRIST AS THE ONLY POSSESSOR AND GIVER OF ETERNAL LIFE

Surah 7:7-9	Moses
7. And verily, We shall recount their whole story with knowledge, for We were never absent (at any time or place).	Genesis 6:5
	And GOD saw that the wickedness of man [was] great in the earth, and [that] every imagination of the thoughts of his heart [was] only evil continually.
8. The balance that day will be true (to nicety): those whose scale (of good) will be heavy, will prosper:	David
	Psalm 14:2;3
9. Those whose scale will be light, will be their souls in perdition, for that they wrongfully treated Our signs.	²The LORD looked down from heaven upon the children of men, to see if there were any that did understand, [and] seek God.
Surah 17:14-15	³ They are all gone aside, they are [all] together become filthy: [there is] none that doeth good, no, not one.
14. (It will be said to him:) "Read thine (own) record: Sufficient is thy soul this day to make out an account against thee."	Isaiah
	Isaiah 53:6
	All we like sheep have gone astray; we have turned every one to his own way; and the LORD hath laid on him the iniquity of us all.

15. Who receiveth guidance, receiveth it for his own benefit: who goeth astray doth so to his own loss: No bearer of burdens can bear the burden of another: nor would We visit with Our Wrath until We had sent an apostle (to give warning). Surah 6:164 164. Say: "Shall I seek for (my) Cherisher other than Allah, when He is the Cherisher of all things (that exist)? Every soul draws the meed of its acts on none but itself: no bearer of burdens can bear of burdens can bear the burden of another. Your goal in the end is towards Allah. He will tell you the truth of the things wherein ye disputed." Surah 23:101-103 101. Then when the Trumpet is blown, there will be no more relationships between them that Day, nor will one ask after another! 102. Then those whose balance (of good deeds) is heavy,- they will attain salvation: 103. But those whose balance is light, will be those who have lost their souls, in Hell will they abide.	Jeremiah Jeremiah 17:9 The heart [is] deceitful above all [things], and desperately wicked: who can know it? Jesus Acts 26:17,18 [17]Delivering thee from the people, and [from] the Gentiles, unto whom now I send thee, [18] To open their eyes, [and] to turn [them] from darkness to light, and [from] the power of Satan unto God, that they may receive forgiveness of sins, and inheritance among them which are sanctified by faith that is in me. Paul Romans 3:23 For all have sinned, and come short of the glory of God;

O nce again we find Mohammed's messages completely contradictory with regard to the writings of the major personalities of the Bible. Again something is fundamentally wrong. The Quran is claiming all men will be judged solely on the heaviness of their good deeds as compared to their bad deeds. There will be no intermediary, advocate, or mediator. The Muslim's salvation will solely depend on his own human effort on doing well. In Surah 53:39, the Quran says **"a man can have nothing but what he strives for."** What a load such a person will carry! Let us examine the implications of the above Quran passages in the life of a committed Muslim who visits the Mosque continually to pray.

In the beginning of each chapter of the Quran, he is told regularly that Allah is most gracious and most merciful. At the same time, he is also told that he will be judged on judgment day solely on his performance on this earth of good deeds outweighing his bad deeds. Until judgment day, he has no way of knowing whether his good deeds have outweighed his bad deeds. Deep within his heart, there is this worry and concern about his fate, especially as he grows older and he gets more anxious not knowing what is going to happen to him after his death. Will he enter paradise or not? In order to increase his good deeds, he strives to pray more and do more good deeds and perhaps give more money to the beggars.

He never stops once to ask himself where Allah's mercy, which is often talked about in Quran is. Where is the mercy if he can only enter paradise based solely on his performance? He goes to pray and submit his will to Allah in the morning as Allah demands of him, but Allah doesn't extend his mercy to him after the prayers in the morning. He then goes back in the afternoon to repeat the prayers and the submission, and again Allah doesn't show him his mercy and keeps telling him through the Quran that he has to wait until the Day of Judgment in order to know his fate.

The process is repeated five times a day and every day of his life. Allah demands so much from him and yet offers him no relief until the Day of Judgment. Remember that as much as he tries everyday to pick up good deeds, he is also picking up bad deeds because he still sins every day. The lies, hatred, anger, and so forth and all the sins that beset the human race are still raging in him. If anything, I will dare even to say that they are increasing because of the restlessness of his soul of not knowing his fate. Just like all other human beings, many Muslims do not want to go hell either! I don't want to go to hell, neither do I want you, the reader, to go to hell.

Though Allah says he is merciful, he never gives Muslims mercy until they close their eyes and give up the ghost. Our spirits and souls don't die; they just depart from the body. Since man has to wait a long time before Resurrection Day, the Muslim soul has to wait a long time before knowing his fate. Where will the soul be? Surely not in heaven and neither in hell because he still doesn't know. I wonder why the Islamic scholars and commentators never reason all these things through. Will his soul will be in purgatory (a concept a faction of Christians believe)?

For the Muslim soul who died since the time of Mohammed, for more than a thousand years, that soul will be living in perpetual fear, worry, and anxiety, not knowing when the day of resurrection will come and what his fate will be until the day of judgment finally arrives. Can you picture billions of Muslims waiting in the queue for their good deeds to be weighted? What a sigh of relief it will be for those whose good deeds are heavier than their bad deeds. But for those whose good deeds are lighter, they will suddenly recognize that Allah's claim to be merciful is empty words. They will now get the revelation that they have been conned all this time. So much has been demanded of them but nothing has been given in return by Allah. My real concern is, will any of the Muslim's good deeds really outweigh their bad deeds to qualify for heaven? Do the facts about the spiritual state of man really support this doctrine in the Quran? Can any human good deeds really be heavier than bad deeds based solely on human effort? I do not think so; neither do I think this is practical.

Humans are so evil in their thoughts, imaginations, and actions. For someone to teach mankind that we can gain heaven's acceptance by doing deeds is totally misleading. I plead with you the non-Christian to reason with me accurately. From the day of Adam and Eve, mankind has sold his will totally and has become rebellious against God. Even when we think we are doing well, our motives can be so wrong. Mankind's life is embedded in gross sin. Our sins are multiple and affect every area of human life.

The Holy Spirit taught us through the prophet Jeremiah that our hearts are desperately wicked, who can grasp the depth of it. The only way we can be delivered from the continuous onslaught of Satan's demons and sin is by a direct intervention from heaven. There is no other way if there has to be a total forgiveness of sins now and not on the Day of Judgment. Psalm 86:5 says "For thou, Lord, [art] good, and ready to forgive; and plenteous in mercy unto all them that call upon thee." God forgives us from the moment we truly repent and ask for forgiveness. We don't have to wait until the Day of Judgment. Unlike the mercy of Allah, the mercy of Jehovah is given from the moment we repent and confess our sins.

I read the story of a Muslim lady who was diagnosed with a terminal sickness and had a very short time to live. She had been a prostitute for the most part of her life and knew that her good deeds were very light. According to her religion it was obvious that she was bound for hell. She approached an Imam and narrated her position to him. She was told by the Imam that by her past behavior, she was bound for hell. She told the Imam that she wanted the mercy of Allah which the Quran so much talked about. She wanted a way out. She wanted Allah to forgive her sins before she dies so that she could be with Allah after death. The Imam reminded her of Surah 53:38-41,

Namely, that no bearer of burdens can bear the burden of another; That man can have nothing but what he strives for; That (the fruit of) his striving will soon come in sight: Then will he be rewarded with a reward complete; That to thy Lord is the final Goal.

The Imam did not have a solution for her. She was eventually introduced to a Christian family who preached to her that the God of the Bible forgives now and assures of salvation now while we still have the breath of live. She repented and committed her life to Jesus. The Lord forgave her and gave her hope and assurance of salvation and peace in her heart. Not long after that she died and went straight to the bosom of the Lord who is truly merciful.

If you are a Muslim reader, I plead with you to seriously reconsider your position in Islam and your relationship with Allah. Why should you worship a god who says to you that he is merciful and yet does not give that mercy now? The Lord Jesus is calling you now. He asks you in Isaiah 55:2, "Why do you spend money for that which is not bread? And your labour for that which satisfies not?" Christ says to you in John 6:51, "I am the living bread which came down from heaven; if anyone eats of this bread, he shall live forever." Christ also says to you, don't hang on to Islam because you were born into it and fear your family. He advises you in Psalm 45:10,11, "forget also thine own people, and thy father's house; so shall the king greatly desire your beauty; for he is Lord; and worship thou him."

The key question in deciding whether Christ is the only possessor and giver of eternal life is first to decide whether man can be righteous based on his merit or not. If man can be righteous on his own merit and be accepted by God based on his own good deeds and merit, then man would not need a savior. But if on the other hand we can conclude that man is incapable of doing good deeds and merit to please God, then man would need a savior and there would be a need for Jesus, and there would be room for Jesus' claim to be the only giver and possessor of eternal life.

So let us now try to reason—is a man a sinner and a chronic one or can he be righteous enough to be accepted by God? The book of Romans, in the first three chapters, argues this case thoroughly and proves that man is a chronic sinner and not only a sinner but depraved. The book of Romans divided the human race into two: the Gentiles and the Jews. In chapter 1 it reasoned that man is guilty of multiple sins and has become foolish and wicked. It ends with a list or catalogue of damnable sins of the gentile nations. He turns on the Jews in Chapter 2. It argues step-by-step that despite holding God's word, the Jews are equally guilty of damnable sins before God. It then concludes in Romans 3:10 *"As it is written, There is none righteous, no, not one":* that popular scripture many Christians love to quote to the world. This third chapter of the book of Romans totally contradicts the above claims of Mohammed in the surahs above that men's good deeds can outweigh their bad deeds to be accepted by God. These two great personalities whose writings have dominated the human race for such a long time are speaking directly opposing messages. Which one of them is speaking the truth? Let us now go to the Bible and find out what some of the prophets left behind for the human race.

God told Moses to write in Genesis 6:5, "And GOD saw that the wickedness of man was great in the earth, and every imagination of the thoughts of his heart was only evil continually." The Lord saw that the wickedness of man was great in the earth and even more importantly, that *every imagination and thought of man's heart was continually abominable*—what a damnable statement God made of the human race! What a contrast between the Jehovah of the Bible and Allah the God of Islam. Again, also between Moses and Mohammed—who is speaking blasphemy?

Another major contrast between the two Gods is found in the Psalms. Please open Psalm 14. In verse 3 of this Psalm it says, *"there is none that doeth good no not one."* Even King David, one of the greatest prophets and kings ever, had a catalog of sins that he struggled with. There is hardly anyone in the Bible who loved God and was totally sold out to God more than he was. In the midst of his passion for God, we see the frailty of the human race. Most great men of God have had some personal issues they have carried and struggled with in their life.

The great prophet Isaiah said in chapter 53, "all we are like sheep have gone astray." Dear reader, I plead with you by the mercies of God that men are evil; men cannot satisfy God's holiness based on their good merits or works. Listen to Jesus when he commissioned Paul in Acts 26:17-18,

Delivering thee from the people, and from the Gentiles, unto whom now I send thee, To open their eyes, and to turn them from darkness to light, and from the power of Satan unto God, that they may receive forgiveness of sins, and inheritance among them which are sanctified by faith that is in me.

Basically, Christ was emphasizing that the Gentile nations, that is, any country outside of Israel, was controlled by Satan. You cannot have a more damaging description of the Gentile nations than what Jesus told Paul. Jesus was saying that all countries outside of Israel, be it China, Africa, Saudi, Russia, or the United States, are all under the clutches and control of Satan. I ask the reader who is speaking blasphemy, Jesus— or Mohammed who says that man can please God by his own deeds.

One other major difference between Islam and Christianity is the issue of sin in children. I cannot tell you how many times I've been questioned by Muslims over the Bible claims which says that children are born in sin and shaped in iniquity and are not born holy and innocent. I have tried to reason without much success with my fellow Muslims that you have to teach children to do good, but you don't have to teach them how to do wrong things. I never realized this major contrast between the two religions until I started preaching to Muslims. They always look bewildered as to how children could have sin in them. Listen to what King David wrote down when he was confessing his sin in Psalm 51:5, 6, *"Behold, I was shapen in iniquity; and in sin did my mother conceive me.* Behold, thou desirest truth in the inward parts: and in the hidden part thou shalt make me to know wisdom."* See also Psalm 58:3.

Sin is a spiritual power that has already permeated the human race. When a child is born, the sin nature is already there. It just does not have the hands and the feet to enforce it or the mouth to speak it out. But the moment the child begins to speak and have control over its limbs, you see the nature of sin being enforced. It therefore becomes clear that parents need to teach children how to do good while doing bad comes naturally.

If you a Muslim reader, I'm not writing to condemn you, but I am asking you to look at the evidence around you. I've said enough to prove to you that we, the human race, are not just sinners, but chronic ones. If we are chronic sinners, then it means we cannot save ourselves and therefore need a savior to save us. It is interesting to note and to recognize that since the world was created there have been many religious readers, philosophers, statesmen, prophets, and preachers of righteousness, but none of these men who have come into this world have claimed to be the only person that forgives us our sins and gives us into eternal life except Christ. Christ stands supreme above all in his claims. He made claims that are exclusive only to him and no one else. The claim in John 14:6, *"Jesus saith unto him, I am the way, the truth, and the life: no man cometh unto the Father, but by me,"* is such a powerful and outstanding claim that it begs belief. That claim is hanging over every human soul, and it is either you take it or leave it. Many times when the Jews were challenging his claims, Jesus constantly told them that had he not done the works that no one had done before, then the Jews were without sin. See also **John 10:37-38.** "If I do not the works of my Father, believe me not. But if I do, though ye believe not me, believe the works: that ye may know, and believe that the Father is in me, and I in him." Christ was basing the truthfulness of his claims on his matchless works.

I plead with you, the Muslim leader, that Jesus is still doing these great works today through his children and preachers around the world. It is not a lack of evidence which is the problem but a lack of interest which stops people searching for this evidence in the world today. There are many Christians who have witnessed these great works and miracles, and if you search hard enough, you will find his miraculous power for yourself.

Chapter 11

THE QURAN'S REJECTION OF CHRIST BUILDING HIS UNIQUE CHURCH IN THE WORLD

Surah 9:33	Psalm 2:6-9
33. It is He Who hath sent His Messenger with guidance and the Religion of Truth, to proclaim it over all religion, even though the Pagans may detest (it).	Yet have I set my king upon my holy hill of Zion.
	I will declare the decree: the LORD hath said unto me, Thou art my Son; this day have I begotten thee.
Surah 48:28	Ask of me, and I shall give [thee] the heathen for thine inheritance, and the uttermost parts of the earth for thy possession.
28. It is He Who has sent His Messenger with Guidance and the Religion of Truth, to proclaim it over all religion: and enough is Allah for a Witness.	Thou shalt break them with a rod of iron; thou shalt dash them in pieces like a potter's vessel.
	Isaiah 9:6, 7
Surah 61:9	For unto us a child is born, unto us a son is given: and the government shall be upon his shoulder: and his name shall be called Wonderful, Counsellor, The mighty God, The everlasting Father, The Prince of Peace.
9. It is He Who has sent His Messenger with Guidance and the Religion of Truth, that he may proclaim it over all religion, even though the Pagans may detest (it).	Of the increase of his government and peace there shall be no end, upon the throne of David, and upon his kingdom, to order it, and to establish it with judgment and with justice from henceforth even for ever. The zeal of the LORD of hosts will perform this.

Isaiah 11:10

And in that day there shall be a root of Jesse, which shall stand for an ensign of the people; to it shall the Gentiles seek: and his rest shall be glorious.

Isaiah 28:1

[16]Therefore thus saith the Lord GOD, Behold, I lay in Zion for a foundation a stone, a tried stone, a precious corner [stone], a sure foundation: he that believeth shall not make haste.

Matthew 16:13-19

[13]When Jesus came into the coasts of Caesarea Philippi, he asked his disciples, saying, Whom do men say that I the Son of man am?
[14] And they said, Some [say that thou art] John the Baptist: some, Elias; and others, Jeremias, or one of the prophets.
[15] He saith unto them, But whom say ye that I am?
[16] And Simon Peter answered and said, Thou art the Christ, the Son of the living God.
[17] And Jesus answered and said unto him, Blessed art thou, Simon Barjona: for flesh and blood hath not revealed [it] unto thee, but my Father which is in heaven.
[18] And I say also unto thee, That thou art Peter, and upon this rock I will build my church; and the gates of hell shall not prevail against it.
[19] And I will give unto thee the keys of the kingdom of heaven: and whatsoever thou shalt bind on earth shall be bound in heaven: and whatsoever thou shalt loose on earth shall be loosed in heaven.

Revelation 7:9;10

After this I beheld, and, lo, a great multitude, which no man could number, of all nations, and kindreds, and people, and tongues, stood before the throne, and before the Lamb, clothed with white robes, and palms in their hands;

And cried with a loud voice, saying, Salvation to our God which sitteth upon the throne, and unto the Lamb.

S urely, again in the words of the Quran, someone is speaking grievous lies. Is it Allah's religion which will prevail over all other religions, or is it Christ whose religion will prevail over all other religions? After the July bombing in London, I spoke to a Sikh who sells spare car parts. He told me that he was neither a Muslim nor a Christian, but he is very grateful for the existence of Christianity in the world. I asked him why? He also has observed that each time Islam rises up its head to try to take over the world, Christianity is always the last hurdle which Islam finds difficult to overcome. He said that as long as Christianity is around, they the rest of mankind, are sure to be delivered from the sword of Islam. That man is not isolated in his thoughts. There are millions who think and believe like him.

The Old Testament is full of many prophecies that Christ will build his church and the church shall endure and overcome all its enemies. Some of the references to these points can be found in the following scriptures: Isaiah 28:16; Psalms 45:6, 7, 17; Isaiah 42:1-8; Daniel 9:24.

In Matthew 16:13-19, when Peter answered Christ enquiries about his identity and affirmed that Christ is the Son of the living God, Jesus congratulated him and said that it was his Father in heaven who revealed the answer to him. Jesus responded with the words **"blessed art thou."** The opposite of that statement is also very true and acts as a warning to the one who does not recognize Christ as the Son of the living God as such a person is in dire straits.

Take note of that word "revealed." We can conclude that anyone that does not believe that Christ is the Son of the living God has not heard from Christ's Father. We know therefore that Christ is not the son of Allah. It stands to reason also that the Allah who inspired Mohammed is not the Father who revealed Christ to Peter. Christ further went on to state that upon this revelation of him as the Son of God, he will build his church and the gates of hell shall not prevail against it. Please take note of the words *"his church."* We can infer from this passage that Christ did not only come to save individuals to take them to heaven but he came to establish a living church. Everyone past or present who have believed in him as Lord and Savior are united in spirit by the Holy Spirit. First Corinthians 12:12 says " For by one Spirit are we all baptized into one body (Christ).

There is a spiritual cord going through everyone who has submitted his will to Christ. The Apostle Paul described this phenomenon wonderfully in Ephesians 2:18-22 that the church is the habitation of God through the Spirit. All those who have put their faith and trust in Christ for their redemption from nation to nation have become the household of God. What a glorious union of hearts knitted together by faith in Christ. Christ's church is not held together by coercion, violence, fear, intimidation, and threats. Listen to the Master giving instructions to his church few days before his departure in John 13:34-35,

A new commandment I give unto you, That ye love one another; as I have loved you, that ye also love one another. By this shall all *men* know that ye are my disciples, if ye have love one to another.

On this issue, Islam stands in no comparison to the church. I personally cannot count how many times I have had Muslims fearful of other Muslims when I engage them in religious discussions. Grown-up adults fearful of other adults in discussing religion? What a sad state of human affairs. Islam is littered with stories of former Muslims living in terror of their own families because they have rejected the faith. There are many Muslims in every land who have secretly abandoned the religion but cannot say so publicly because of the fear or threat to their life. This threat of physical harm by other Muslims is one of the main reasons why Muslim numbers are not significantly reduced.

Unfortunately, there are many people around the world who ignorantly claim that the two camps of Christianity and Islam are the same. The two camps are not the same. The Bible says that the camp of Jesus Christ is the household of God; therefore, any camp that does not acknowledge that Jesus is the Son of the living God and violently opposes the revelation of him as Son of God, cannot come from the God who is the Father of Jesus Christ.

Looking at verse 18 of Matthew 16, Christ makes another claim that the gates of hell shall not prevail against his church. This statement implies that there will be a violent and continuous confrontation between the church and the gates of hell. The **"gates of hell"** stands for everything that is evil and satanic. The emphasis goes beyond the human race. There are unseen forces seeking to destroy and violently oppose the growth of the church. The verse further implies that the conflict and struggle will never end. However, it also assures the church that, in the midst of all the hostilities and onslaught of Satan on the church, it will never be diminished or destroyed. Since the Quran continually persists that Christ is not the son of Allah as we have mentioned in previous chapters, it stands to reason looking at verse 18 that the message of the Quran is included in the powers that will not prevail against the church.

When one reads the above surahs where the Quran claims Islam will prevail against all other religions, the only enemies mentioned in them is the phrase "though the Pagans may desist it."

Unlike the claims of Christ, Satan is not mentioned in the quranic claims. This fact makes me highly suspicious of this quranic claim. Can you imagine a religion prevailing over every other religion without Satan's involvement in opposing that religion? I doubt it! Think with me.

I plead with you, the Muslim reader, do not be angry with me or any person you find reading or promoting this book. These passages are both in the Quran and in the Bible. They will be there long after we've gone. We the human race are being taken for a ride by one of these two great religions, and we have a duty for own piece of mind and sanity to get to the bottom of this.

Christ claims of success for his church went beyond success against Satan, demons, and hell. He further promised them the keys to the Kingdom of heaven and with the keys comes authority to bind and loose in both earth and heaven. Please take another look at the above surahs and the verses from the Bible. Contrast the two personalities speaking. Which of the two is speaking with authority and absolute power: Allah or Yahweh, Mohammed or Christ, Quran or the Bible?

Try to perceive in your heart what is being stated in these verses. Christ is giving his church an awesome responsibility and power. These verses tell us that Christ has faith in his church and that his church will perform. Look at secularism in the western countries and how they are hiding behind appeasing different faiths. They aim to oppose and drive out Christianity from western countries. But the truth is that they are not able to silence the church because the words of Christ are true and will continually prevail.

It is very interesting to watch the affairs of the western countries and how secularism hides behind Islam to push its agenda. It pretends to be the guardians of fairness in religious affairs, pretending to care for Muslims and other faiths rights while in truth it is determined to replace Christianity with secularism. They totally ignore the fact that Muslims and other faiths make up of only a small percentage of the population in western countries. Suddenly, we are told Christians ought to be good boys, that they shouldn't offend the Muslims living among them. These same intellectuals do not write to Islamic countries asking them not to offend the Christians living among them. The balance is always shifted in the hearts and minds against the Christian faith. We Christian leaders know who is pushing the buttons.

When we read the Surahs in the passages above, we see Mohammed clearly stating that his religion will prevail over all the other religions, including Christianity. He is sure of his words. The Son of God, too, is also sure of his words. The battle for souls is constantly waging, and we men are caught in this spiritual battle between these two great men. Both camps are fully determined to win the spiritual struggle. Christ further told us of how his church would behave on the earth, and how they should aim to behave. He said to them in Matthew 5:13-16

Ye are salt of the earth: but if the salt have lost his savour, wherewith shall it be salted? it is thenceforth good for nothing, but to be cast out, and to be trodden under foot of men

14 Ye are the light of the world. A city that is set on a hill cannot be hid.

15 Neither do men light a candle, and put it under a bushel, but on a candlestick; and it giveth light unto all that are in the house.

16 Let your light so shine before men, that they may see your good works, and glorify your Father which is in heaven.

In Luke 6:27-28, he gave his church further instructions. "He said "love your enemies, do good to those that hate you; bless them that curse you and pray for them that despitefully use you." What a contrast of instructions Mohammed gave to his followers in Surah 9:29-31,

Fight those who believe not in Allah nor the Last Day, nor hold that forbidden which hath been forbidden by Allah and His Messenger, nor acknowledge the religion of Truth, (even if they are) of the People of the Book, until they pay the Jizya with willing submission, and feel themselves subdued.

30. The Jews call 'Uzair a son of Allah, and the Christians call Christ the son of Allah. That is a saying from their mouth; (in

this) they but imitate what the unbelievers of old used to say. Allah.s curse be on them: how they are deluded away from the Truth!

31. They take their priests and their anchorites to be their lords in derogation of Allah, and (they take as their Lord) Christ the son of Mary; yet they were commanded to worship but One Allah. there is no god but He. Praise and glory to Him: (Far is He) from having the partners they associate (with Him).

It is interesting to note that, the work of Christ and the church was prophesied to Adam and Eve in the garden when they sinned. Let's read it in Genesis 3:15, "And I will put enmity between thee and the woman, and between thy seed and her seed; it shall bruise thy head, and thou shalt bruise his heel."

In Genesis 3:15, Christ is described as "the seed of the woman (virgin birth)" and we are informed that, there will be a continuing conflict between the seed of Satan and "the seed of the woman." It shall be an unending conflict, and the seed of the woman will triumph over the seed of the serpent although the seed of the serpent will inflict a form of damage on the seed of the woman. Though "the seed of the woman" (Christ) destroyed Satan through death on the cross (Hebrews 2:14), the victory is enforced by the church of Christ through the preaching of the gospel.

Isaiah confirmed the virgin birth in Isaiah 7:14 and further tells us in Isaiah 9:6-7 that Christ will have a church. He described that church as "his government." This government (the church) rules both the political and spiritual affairs of the nations. It is the prayers of the church that controls the affairs of the nations. Verse 7 says,

[7]Of the increase of [his] government and peace [there shall be] no end, upon the throne of David, and upon his kingdom, to order it, and to establish it with judgment and with justice from henceforth even for ever. The zeal of the LORD of hosts will perform this. This statement is identical to the words Jesus used in Matthew 16:18. The Old Testament is littered with so many prophecies about Christ's church and about his coming to establish his church in the world. See the following scriptures: Isaiah 42:1-10; 49:1-10; 61:1-3.

In the book of Revelation, we have prophecies that will remain until the end of times. Right in the heart of the book of Revelation is the church of Jesus Christ. The Book of Revelation is a wondereful book. The church together with the angels will rapture in praises and joy as Christ takes the book and looses the seals in chapter 5. In chapter 7 the church is described wonderfuly as a great multitude which no one could number. The church is dressed in white robes, and the Bible says their clothes have been washed in the blood of the lamb. This is a wonderful sight to behold. Glory to the lamb that was slain so that they could be redeemed. The church of Jesus Christ will live forever and prevail over all other reglions so that men may receive eternal life and find themselves in heaven. If you are a Muslim reader, don't shun the book of Revelation; it contains wonderful descriptions of the church. All are welcome to join.

Chapter 12

THE QURAN'S REJECTION OF THE HOLY SPIRIT

I slam is riddled with confusion on the identity of the Holy Spirit. The Muslim theologians are at a loss in explaining what the Holy Spirit is. There is also much confusion among the average Muslims, as well. Again the source of the confusion is from the Quran. The words "Holy Spirit" actually appear in the Quran together with different definitions of what the "Holy Spirit" is. The following verses and surahs illustrate my point.

In Surah 15:29, "When I have fashioned him (in due proportion) and breathed into him of My spirit, fall ye down in obeisance unto him." Compare this surah to Genesis 2:7, "And the LORD God formed man [of] the dust of the ground, and breathed into his nostrils the breath of life; and man became a living soul." It is clear in comparing Surah 15:29 with Genesis 2:7 that Mohammed is confusing "breath of Life" with "My spirit." Throughout the Bible, when God uses the phrase "My Spirit," he is usually referring to the Holy Spirit as in Genesis 6:3, "And the Lord said, My spirit will not always strive with man." "My spirit" here in Genesis 6:3 is a person. You can deduce he is a person because of the word strive, which is an action word.

If you ask over a thousand Muslim scholars and commentators to explain what "My spirit" means in Surah 15:29, you will have many different opinions. Please look carefully at Surah 15:29. Is it confusing to you?

"She placed a screen (to screen herself) from them; then We sent her our angel, and he appeared before her as a man in all respects" (Surah 19:17) "He sent to her our angel." That angel mentioned is believed by many Muslims that it is the angel Gabriel. Other Muslims believe that this angel Gabriel is the Holy Spirit.

"Christ Jesus the son of Mary was (no more than) an apostle of Allah, and His Word, which He bestowed on Mary, and a spirit proceeding from Him" (Surah 4:171). Jesus is described here as "His word which he bestowed on Mary and a Spirit proceeding from Him (Allah)"

Aren't these Surahs confusing to you the reader? Muslims are told repeatedly in the Quran that Jesus Christ is not divine. But Surah 4:171 suggests that he is divine. Also, the Holy Spirit is being confused with Jesus. Contrast the above surah with a corresponding passage from the Bible. Luke 1:35 says, "And the angel answered and said unto her, The Holy Ghost shall come upon thee, and the power of the Highest shall overshadow thee: therefore also that holy thing which shall be born of thee shall be called the Son of God." Look at how clearly the Bible passage is compared to the above surah.

In Surah 4:171, it appears that Jesus is being called a spirit from Allah. There is a lack of clarity here, and if you ask different Muslim scholars, they are unable to agree on the exact meaning.

Among all the different views held by Muslims on the identity of the Holy Spirit, the most prevalent and strongly held view is that the Holy Spirit is Mohammed himself. On many occasions, to support their position, my Muslim friends have pointed to the scriptures in the Bible which make reference to the prophecies from Jesus about the coming of the Holy Spirit on the disciples, especially in the Gospel of John. They continually claim that all those passages in which the Holy Spirit was mentioned were in direct reference to the advent of Mohammed and not the Holy Spirit. The source of this constant assertion by Muslims is a direct result of a verse in the Quran (Surah 61:6). In Surah61:6, many Muslims assert that Mohammed claimed to be the Holy Spirit Jesus promised to send to the disciples after his ascension to heaven

And remember, Jesus, the son of Mary, said: "O Children of Israel! I am the apostle of Allah (sent) to you, confirming the Law (which came) before me, and giving Glad Tidings of an Messenger to come after me, whose name shall be Ahmad." But when he came to them with Clear Signs, they said, "this is evident sorcery!" And remember, Jesus, the son of Mary, said: "O Children of Israel! I am the apostle of Allah (sent) to you, confirming the Law (which came) before me, and giving Glad Tidings of an Messenger to come after me, whose name shall be Ahmad." But when he came to them with Clear Signs, they said, "this is evident sorcery! (Surah 61:6)

This verse in the Quran is very widely known among Muslims and much of their literature is littered with this verse.

My Muslim friend, whom I have been referring to, loved to quote it. He also knew all the biblical passages in the Gospel of John referring to the coming of the Holy Spirit. Some of the passages are John 14:16-18, 26; John 15:26; John 16:7-8; 12-14. In all the numerous times I have heard him quote these passages, not once did I hear him quote the remainder of John in Chapters 14-16. In typical Islamic fashion, he is not interested in any part of the Gospel of John. When men can behave so impudently, there is not much you can do with them except to pray to the Lord to have mercy on their souls.

In a recent seminar I held, I mentioned that Mohammed claimed in the Quran to be the comforter which Jesus promised to the disciples who should come after him. I further said that almost every Muslim knows that claim is in the Quran, while the Christian hardly knows that the Quran teaches this. There was a pastor at the meeting, who felt very alarmed that after almost twenty-five years of being a Christian, she didn't know that the Quran taught that Mohammed is the Holy Spirit Jesus promised was to come after his ascension, and neither had any Christian leader told her that. Her exact words were "how could almost every Muslim know that Mohammed claimed to be the Holy Spirit and I a Christian leader didn't know this?" I mention this to give you a picture of the scale of apathy among Christians.

Unfortunately, not many Christians have any desire whatsoever to learn anything about Islam. When the question is put to the Christian many of them say—"just preach Christ and it will be enough." They forget that the preaching of Christ involved also referring to his enemies. In the Gospel of John, Christ was continuously having a go at his religious enemies.

155

John 10 is mainly about the religious enemies who have established huge world religions, competing with him for the souls of men. He called them thieves and robbers. Christ didn't ignore them; he confronted them.

Sometimes, I have heard other pastors say that we should focus on the miracles, healings, and signs and wonders, and that this will be sufficient to convert the Muslims. Where then is the teaching and the preaching? I personally know Muslims who have seen the miracles of Christ at Christian meetings and still attribute the healings to Allah. We need all the tools for the work. Miracles, signs, and wonders will get some saved, but not all will be saved that way and therefore we need the use of all the tools of the gospel, that is, the taught word, signs, miracles, wonders, and the good works, as well, to get the job done.

In all the denials and blasphemies I have read in the Quran concerning the rejection of Christ as Lord and Savior, the worst one is Mohammed claiming to be the Holy Spirit. Jesus said in Matthew 12:31-32, "Wherefore I say unto you, All manner of sin and blasphemy shall be forgiven unto men: but the blasphemy against the Holy Spirit shall not be forgiven unto men."

It is bad enough to suggest in the Quran that the Holy Spirit is the angel of Gabriel or God's breath; however, it is much worse to actually claim in the Quran that, he, Mohammed, is the Holy Spirit. It frightens me to think of the consequences of his claims. His claims beg belief. When the Holy Spirit moved over the surface of the deep in Genesis 1:2, was Mohammed around? Where was Mohammed when God said to Jesus and the Holy Spirit in Genesis 1:26, "Let us make man in our own image," the Holy Spirit is continuously mentioned in the Bible as being directly involved in directing the affairs of the universe from the beginning of creation up to now. For a mere man who died (and with his bones still buried in the grave), to come up with such a monstrous claim is scary. For you, the Muslim, who is convinced of his claims while his bones are still buried in the ground, take heed; the Holy Spirit is waiting to judge you.

The Holy Spirit is none of what the Quran suggests he is. He is a person and a third member of the blessed triune God. He is the one who convicts sinners to believe Jesus to be saved. The Holy Spirit is not the angel Gabriel; he is not God's active force or power as Jehovah Witnesses believe; he is not a cloud of air; he is definitely not Mohammed; he is not even Jesus. The word Spirit means a being with own faculties of intellect, will, and power; only as humans, our naked eyes can't see him. Many times we are told in the Bible that he makes decisions and does things by his will and power, as in 1 Corinthians 12:11, "But all these worketh that one and the selfsame Spirit, dividing to every man severally as *he will.*" In this verse he decides whom he gives his power and gifts to.

My Spiritual Journey into the Christianity/Islam Debate

About thirty years ago, I used to believe in the existence of God but had no understanding in the differences in the religions. At that time all that mattered to me was to believe that God existed or that there is a creator. I used to think that whether one was a Jew, Christian, Muslim, or Sikh, it was irrelevant insofar as one believed that there was a creator.

At the time I used to work with people from different religions. I used to see in many factories, Islamic quotations of the Quran posted at different work places. I used to see the word Allah often and many times saw the word God written in brackets alongside Allah. Because I saw the names Allah and God side-by-side for many years, I used to think that they were the same, and that Allah just meant God in the Arabic language. Unfortunately there are many people in the world who believe the same as I did thirty years ago. I was totally ignorant of the deep spiritual struggle among the religions to control human beings.

Something eventually happened that changed my whole perception and understanding about the religions. I owned a ladies clothes factory employing people. One of the employees was a Christian called Clara. She was a gospel fanatic and constantly preached to all of us, inviting me in particular to church. After nearly a whole year I went to church with my late wife. After the service, the pastor surprisingly announced, *"Don't read the Quran it is a forgery."* He didn't tell us why the Quran is a forgery. He just said don't read it. This pronouncement from the pastor was a wakeup call for me. I asked myself how could the Quran be a forgery when I had always seen the word God written alongside Allah in the factories and had also heard the Muslims declaring that they also believed in God just as the Christians do? *How could two groups both claim to believe in God and one of them be a forgery or wrong? How could Islam be wrong when they are repeatedly declaring to believe in God?* I kept repeating these questions to myself over and over again. Maybe I didn't hear him properly, I would often say to myself. How could over a billion souls claiming to believe in God be wrong? If you are a Christian preacher to Muslims, have you encountered this question before in sharing your faith with Muslims?

For the first time in my life, I was confronted with serious issues much bigger than my narrow blind views I had. I was about thirty-five years old and lived in my own dream world of ignorance, foolishness, and lack of interest in spiritual things. I was totally unaware of the deep spiritual struggle being waged relentlessly around me among the religions of the world. Oh, how many people are in such spiritual darkness around the world? Untold millions if not billions are living in total darkness and have no knowledge that heaven and hell are locked in a fierce spiritual conflict continually for the hearts of men. I see them across the nations, seas, languages, peoples, tribes, and cities. They are scattered across the four corners of the earth. They are like sheep without a shepherd. Who will take my testimony to them and tell them how I was once lost and totally unaware of the spiritual struggles behind religions? Perchance some may wake up from their spiritual slumber when they hear my testimony and begin to be concerned about which religion is true.

I am by nature a curious person and like to read. I was intrigued by that proclamation *"Don't read the Quran it is forgery."* All week long I wanted to know why it is forgery. I kept saying to myself I just wish the pastor could tell us why the Quran is a forgery. Come the following Sunday I couldn't wait to get back to the church to hear a little more about this strange belief. Again, at the end of the service, the pastor made the same proclamation without giving us a reason why the Quran is forgery.

I went back subsequent weeks only to hear the same declarations without explanations. After few weeks I went to the Islamic bookshop and bought a book on the life history of Mohammed, the prophet of Islam. I went for his life history before the Quran because I reasoned that if the religion he has left behind is forgery according to the pastor, there would be evidence of wrongdoing in his personal life. My reasoning proved to be right. There were many things in the prophet of Allah's personal life that gave me concern. After another few weeks I went to buy the Quran itself. In fact, I was so curious in finding out what was in it that I stopped my van few times to read the Quran. I just wanted to know why I was being told not to read it. I got hold of the Bible and started comparing the two religious books.

At that time, I had a close friend who was a Muslim. I told him about what I was hearing about his religion from the pastor. It didn't take long before he went on the offensive against the pastor and Christianity on the whole. He started quoting many passages from the Bible, using them to attack the Christian faith. I started gathering literature from both the Christians and the Muslims to compare and contrast the two religions. I also started talking to the people in the two religions. It didn't take me long to find out that the two leading world religions had major and irreconcilable beliefs. I also quickly found out that my Muslim friend was constantly misquoting the Bible, and whenever he got the quote right, he misinterpreted it or misapplied it. I also found that most of the Muslim literature were giving out the same misinformation about the Christian faith. *It was the Muslim's error of misquoting the Bible and attacking the*

Christian faith that eventually led me to make a decisive move towards Christ.

Soon after giving my life to Christ, I got drawn to the ongoing spiritual debate between the two religions. I began making a conscious effort to bring the discussions of the two religions on the agenda everywhere I went. I started taking the side for Christ. The more I talked to both Christians and Muslims, the more I loved Christ and found out that the Muslims are desperately in need of their Savior. Sometimes Christians think Jesus is only for them. The whole world needs Christ. He died for the sins of the whole world.

As time went on I got more involved in the ongoing debates and started becoming passionate for the gospel and especially reaching the Muslims. Hardly a day went past without sharing my faith with a Muslim. The more I spoke to them the more I was learning fast about their religion and how they differ from the Christian faith. The Spirit of Christ took control of my soul and filled me with deep love for people without Christ, especially Muslims. Much later I started making inquiries about other religions as well as Islam. I learnt that the Jews hold the same Old Testament as the Christians. In other to verify that, I went and got the Old Testament translated by Jewish rabbis who were not Christians, to compare it with what the Christians are holding. I found it to be the same, literally word-for-word, except few places where they didn't want to highlight passages that the Christians are claiming to refer to Jesus. I still have the Jewish translation called Tanakh with me. Compare the Jewish rabbis' translation of the last verse in Psalm 2 with the King James translation of the same verse.

Rabbis' Translation

Pay homage in good faith, least He be angered, and your way be doomed in the mere flash of his anger.

Happy are all who take refuge in Him.

King James translation

Kiss the Son, lest He be angry, and ye perish from the way, when his wrath is kindled but a little. Blessed are all they that put their trust in Him.

Have you noticed any difference between the two translations? To really understand the differences in the two translations you need to study the whole Psalm, taking particular notice of verses 2 and 7. There are two separate persons described as divine in these verses. One is the Father who is described as the LORD in verse 2, and the other is called the Son in verse 7 and in verse 2 called the Christ.

When one reads the rabbis' translation, it is confusing trying to figure out whether the person being referred to in verse 12 is the Father or the Son. On the hand, the King James Version makes it quite clear that it is the Son the Bible is referring to. Also take note of the difference between the words **"Happy"** and **"blessed."** Interesting enough, the rest of the translation in Psalm 2 in the two versions are identical. It is only when it came to Christ we find little adjustments here and there. Also it is in the presence of these minor adjustments in the translations that the Muslims accuse the Christians and the Jews of corrupting the scriptures. I have already tackled these charges and stated that the manuscripts are the same while the translations can have minor differences, subject to the translators' understanding. I also mentioned that similar problems exist with the Quran translations.

I narrated the differences in the two translations to inform you that I delved deep into the religious debate with much reading and research. I was not satisfied with superficiality. My soul wanted to know more about Jesus and also his spiritual enemies he called thieves and robbers in John 10.

After about two years after my conversion I informed my church that I believed God was calling me to be an evangelist. They took me to Speaker's Corner and gave me a soapbox to stand on to preach. Suddenly I was surrounded by many people, most of them Muslims. I was thrust into a new era of Christianity/Islam debate. I will continue my testimony on Christianity/Islam debate in my next book. God bless you for reading through this book. More than half of the world's population life depends on these two great religions; please take this subject serious and do not only read but study them.

If you are a non-Christian reading this book, please change your mind about Jesus and ask him to save you from your sins. Just pray a simple prayer asking him to save you. He will answer you and save you, and you will know it. Thank the Father for giving us his only Son to give us eternal life. Tell the Father that you believe His Son Jesus died for your sins and rose again from the dead and lives forevermore. Tell the Holy Spirit to come and dwell inside you and have fellowship with you. God will save you as you pray and believe. Amen.

BIBLIOGRAPHY

G J O Mosha, *Who is this Allah* Dorchester House publications, Gerrards Cross,

Bucks SL9 8HA, UK June 2004

Don Richardson *Secrets of the Koran* Regal Books, Ventura, California, US 2003

Yousuf Saleem Chishti, Aleemiyah Memorial Series, *What is Christianity* World Federation of Islamic Missions

Patrick Sookhdeo, *The Challenge of Islam to the Church and its Mission*

Isaac Publishing, 6729 Curran Street, McLean VA 22101. US 2009

Patrick Sookdheo, *Understanding Islamic Terrorism* Isaac Publishing, The Old Rectory

River Street, Pewsey, Wiltshire, SN9 5DB, UK. 2004

Patrick Sookhdeo, *A Christian's Pocket Guide to Islam* Isaac Publishing, The Old Rectory

River Street, Pewsey, Wiltshire, SN9 5DB, UK 2001

F.S. Copleston *Christ or Mohammed? The Bible or the Koran.* Nuprint Ltd, 30b Station Road

Harpenden, Herts, AL5 4SE 1989

Dr Anis A Shorrosh, *Islam Revealed, A Christian Arab's View of Islam* Thomas Nelson

Publishers, Nashville, Tennessee, US 1988

Samuel M Zwemer, *The Muslim Christ*, The Message for Muslims Trust. 1912

G.J.O. Moshay, *How We Found Jesus—20 Ex-Muslims Testify*

Ergun Mehmet Caner & Emir Fethi Caner *Unveiling Islam* Kregel Publications

PO Box 2607, Grand Rapids, MI 49501 2002

Abdiyah Akbar Abdul-Haqq, *Sharing Your Faith with a Muslim,* Bethany House Publishers, Minneapolis, Minnesota 1980